TWO SHORT PLAYS

TWO SHORT PLAYS

By Ioana Cornea and Benjamin Goluboff

LAKE FOREST
COLLEGE

ACKNOWLEDGMENTS

Funding for this edition of *Two Short Plays* comes in part from Digital Chicago: Unearthing History and Culture, a four-year (2015-2018) grant at Lake Forest College from The Andrew W. Mellon Foundation. Digital Chicago seeks to unearth Chicago's forgotten history and preserve it for a digital future, through coursework, innovative digital humanities projects, and urban archaeology. For more information, visit lakeforest.edu/digitalchicago or digital-chicago.org

This edition first published 2016 by
Lake Forest College Press.

Lake Forest College
555 N. Sheridan Road
Lake Forest, IL 60045

lakeforest.edu/andnow

© 2016 Lake Forest College Press

Lake Forest College Press publishes in the broad spaces
of Chicago studies. Our imprint, &NOW Books, publishes
innovative and conceptual literature and serves as the
publishing arm of the &NOW writers' conference and
organization.

ISBN: ISBN 978-1-941423-94-3

Book and cover design by Jaime Deare. "The Wonder Hat"
drawings by Jaime Deare. "Back of the Yards" drawings by
Emily Murman.

Printed in the United States

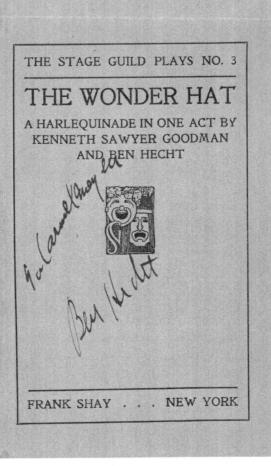

THE STAGE GUILD PLAYS NO. 3

THE WONDER HAT

A HARLEQUINADE IN ONE ACT BY
KENNETH SAWYER GOODMAN
AND BEN HECHT

FRANK SHAY . . . NEW YORK

Title page for "The Wonder Hat" title page signed by
co-author Hecht. Photo courtesy The Newberry Library,
Chicago (Call no. MMS Goodman, Box 8, Folder 341).

"To Restore the Old Visions and to Win the New"

In 1916, Kenneth Sawyer Goodman and Ben Hecht's short play "The Wonder Hat" debuted, along with more well-known works of American literature such as Eugene O'Neill's fourth play, *Now I Ask You*; Robert Frost's *Mountain Interval*, Ezra Pound's *Lustra*, and Carl Sandburg's *Chicago Poems*. Not a central work of American literature, or even of Chicago literature of the period, "The Wonder Hat," and "Back of the Yards"†(which Goodman wrote in 1914 without Hecht's collaboration) claim our attention for a variety of good reasons.

Both plays illustrate the themes and the *modus operandi* of the Little Theater movement, of which Goodman was a central backer and something of a theorist. "Back of the Yards," especially, demonstrates the social vision of the Little Theater Movement and its connections to the social reform program of the Settlement Houses. "The Wonder Hat" has a certain stylistic charisma as its work changes on a traditional scheme from the *commedia dell' arte* tradition. Both plays register, in engagingly different ways,†what it meant to be "modern" in Chicago during the Woodrow Wilson years. Finally, both plays derive from the imagination of the man in honor of whom one of Chicago's most distinguished theaters was named.

The plot of "The Wonder Hat" follows the *commedia dell' arte* convention of star-crossed lovers overcoming obstacles to their union. Magical objects — a hat that confers invisibility and a slipper that makes its wearer irresistible to men — create comic confusions.†Hecht and Goodman's script brings to this traditional framework an atmosphere or tone that their 1916 audiences would have recognized as modern.

For example, when Punchinello, the fifth-business figure†who will provide the lovers with the magic objects, first comes on stage, he cries "new loves for old," and offers a menu of those cast-off items he's willing to take in trade: "rejected poems, unfinished plays, bottles, bookmarks, and worn-out religions."†When Harlequin and Pierrot first make their appearance they are presented as world-weary boulevardiers "swinging light canes with an air of elegant ennui." Their first exchange establishes the play's *mise en scene* as an absurdist roundabout:

> HARLEQUIN. [*Indicating with a wave of his cane*] Dear fellow, this is a circular path. It runs quite around the outer edge of the park. It delights me. I always spend my evenings here. One can walk for hours with the absolute certainty of never getting anywhere.

> PIERROT. [*Removing his eyeglass*] Dear chap, in these days of suburban progress, I had not supposed such a place possible.

Hecht and Goodman's audiences would have recognized the atmosphere conjured on this stage as one consistent with a dry-eyed, unsentimental skepticism that many of them would have called modern. The drama of "The Wonder Hat" showed that, even for moderns thus construed, love could still triumph.

In contrast, "Back of the Yards" configures its modernity differently. Rather than a world in which ideals have come to a stylized exhaustion and characters enact an elegant ennui; in this world realistically drawn characters come to grief in the impoverished neighborhoods behind the Stockyards and dedicated reformers seek a remedy for familiar social ills. Granted, without Hecht's collaboration, Goodman's dialogue is creaky – many of the principals here sound like the stage Irish they are. The uptown Goodman had a largely theoretical understanding of the south side, and his "Back of the Yards" neighborhood has a somewhat abstract quality. But the issue with which his characters grapple—juvenile crime—was very much of the moment, and was as much a part of the dialogue at Jane Addams's Hull House as it was on Goodman's stage.

The program Goodman's Father Vincent offers to reduce juvenile crime is, admittedly, somewhat hazy:

> PRIEST.   But it's not graft or politics I'm thinking of. There's something does more to send boys and girls to hell then either of them. It's the rule-of-thumb way we go at crime for the most part, making a great bother of catching and punishing the old hands at the game and letting slip the little things, slurring them over, hushing them up, passing by all the sprees and gambling and devilment that give the crook his start.

Goodman appears to have believed with Jane Addams that the theater itself could serve as a weapon against juvenile crime. "Back of the Yards" functioned both as a mouthpiece for Progressive reform (however inexactly conceived), and as a diversion to keep young Chicagoans off the streets and out of trouble.

This edition presents "The Wonder Hat," still Goodman's best-known play, and "Back of the Yards," still interesting for its social vision and reform agenda, with original illustrations by Jaime Deare and Emily Murman, respectively. This brief introduction illustrates the plays' context, genesis and performance history, through brief biographies of Goodman and Hecht, a description of the Little Theater Movement, and a note on the *commedia dell' arte* tradition.

Kenneth Sawyer Goodman

Born in 1883 as the only child of a wealthy Chicago lumber family, Kenneth Sawyer Goodman attended The Hill School in Pottstown, Pennsylvania, where he wrote for *The Hill News*.[1] Later, at Princeton University, he continued writing and editing the University's paper, *The Princeton Tiger*, as well as the *Nassau Literary Review*, and was encouraged by Dean Christian Gauss to pursue his interest in writing for the theater. Goodman graduated from Princeton in 1906 and turned down an offer to teach English at the university, in order to fulfill his obligations as an only child to the family lumber business.[2] In 1912, Goodman married Marjorie Robbins, the daughter of a prominent Chicago attorney. Marjorie served as treasurer of the Chicago Junior League, for which she also organized classes on contemporary political questions ("Cupid in Chicago"). The couple had a daughter, named Marjorie after her mother.

In early 1910, Goodman joined the Cliff Dwellers Club, an elite society of artists and patrons of the arts, founded by novelist Hamlin Garland in 1907. There, Goodman met and collaborated with Thomas Wood Stevens, who would later organize the first collegiate degree-granting Department of Drama in the country

Kenneth Sawyer Goodman with Marjorie Sawyer Goodman, 1917.
Photo courtesy The Newberry Library, Chicago
(Call no. MMS Goodman, Box 8, Folder 346).

at the Carnegie Institute of Technology and become the first director of the Goodman Theater.[3] Goodman and Stevens wrote several short plays, including "The Masque of Montezuma," which they intended for a site-specific performance on the steps of the Art Institute. Goodman and Stevens founded Stage Guild Publications, which published Goodman's plays, solo works, and collaborations for the rest of the decade.

In late 1913, Goodman began collaborating with Ben Hecht, then a twenty-one-year old newspaper reporter, who shared the playwright's interest in the plight of Chicago's immigrant working class. Hecht, who had a passion for writing about the gory details of Chicago crime, would soon become one of Hollywood's most prominent screenwriters. Goodman and Hecht wrote eight one-act plays together, including "The Wonder Hat," "The Hero of Santa Maria," and "An Idyll of the Shops." "Idyll" focused on Jewish life in Chicago garment factories; "Hero" featured an unscrupulous family trying to secure the death benefit for a son who had not in fact died during the war. In addition, they wrote several scripts that depict immigrant Jewish parent-child relationships gone awry. As the first-generation Jewish American characters in these plays attend prestigious schools and become assimilated, they lose respect for the parents who worked hard to give them the opportunities they lacked themselves. The typescripts of these unpublished plays are found at the Newberry Library and include "The Poem of David," "The Egg and the Hen," and "The Home Coming."

In 1916, Hecht connected Goodman to the Players' Workshop, an amateur theater on Chicago's South Side,

Cover for Goodman's play "The Masque of Montezuma."
Photo courtesy The Newberry Library, Chicago
(Call no. MMS Goodman, Box 7, Folder 333).

which was primarily interested in new plays written by Chicago playwrights. Theater historian Stuart Hecht writes that Ben Hecht believed Goodman was a key shaper of the Chicago theater community, as he brought "people from different circles together, encouraging collaborative creative effort".[4] One sees this pattern in the wide range of people with whom Goodman associated, from Hecht, the bohemian journalist, to Thomas Wood Stevens, the patrician academic, as well as his involvement with the elite Cliff Dwellers and the more working-class Players' Workshop.

Goodman also volunteered at the Art Institute and became the director of its Department of Prints.[5] As the First World War approached, Goodman became increasingly involved with war efforts and enlisted in the Navy, taking a staff position at the Great Lakes Naval Training Center in Chicago's northern suburbs. In the fall of 1918, attending a Navy football game, he contracted influenza and became, according to some sources, a victim of the global pandemic of 1918.[6] *The American National Biography*, on the other hand, claims that Goodman caught a cold, which developed into fatal pneumonia.[7] Though some uncertainty exists of the exact cause, Goodman died days after turning 35.

Playwright, director, actor, and financial supporter of Chicago's Little Theater movement, Goodman's legacy lives on in the Goodman Theater endowed by his parents in 1925, in his plays, and in his contribution to the Little Theater Movement. His philosophy is carved above the doorway to the Goodman Theater: "To restore the old visions and to win the new."

Lieut. K. S. Goodman, Moffett's Aid, Dead

Lieutenant Kenneth Sawyer Goodman, aid to Captain W. A. Moffett, commandant at Great Lakes station, died yesterday of pneumonia.

Obituary for Kenneth Sawyer Goodman.
Photo courtesy The Newberry Library, Chicago
(Call no. MMS Goodman, Box 6, Folder 281).

Ben Hecht

Kenneth Sawyer Goodman's collaborator on "The Wonder Hat," as well as a handful of additional one-act plays, published and in manuscript, is better known than the playwright himself, especially to Chicagoans. Ben Hecht was born to immigrant Russian Jewish parents in 1894 on the Lower East Side of Manhattan. His family moved while he was still young to Racine, Wisconsin, where he graduated from Racine High School in 1910. Hecht left for Chicago in that year, where he found work as a picture stealer, selling to Chicago newspapers the photographs of people killed in city accidents – photographs Hecht acquired from the victims' families by a variety of devious strategies.[8] As a cub reporter, Hecht covered crime for the *Chicago Journal* and then joined the staff at *Chicago Daily News* in 1914.

At the *Daily News* Hecht initially covered crime, then post-war life in Berlin, and eventually wrote a celebrated column registering impressions of urban life in the developing metropolis. *1001 Afternoons in Chicago* contained vignettes about Chicago crime, trial scenes, romances, marriage, as well as impressions of the lake and lakeshore.[9] The column combined the nineteenth-century traditions of the *flaneur* and the sketch, filtering kaleidoscopic images of the city through a detached and ironic sensibility in a prose piece of one or two pages. The *Chicago Daily News* fired Hecht in 1922 over a censorship scandal about *Fantazius Mallare*, a work of stylized erotica Hecht wrote in collaboration with Wallace Smith, a Hearst reporter who drew in the style of Aubrey Beardsley.[10] Hecht's writing and Smith's drawings were considered too obscene for a society

Ben Hecht, 1919.
Photo by Culver Pictures, courtesy of Wikimedia commons.

that was still very much concerned with prohibiting vice from the marketplace. Fired from the *Daily News*, Hecht turned to writing novels, plays, and screenplays. Around this time, he founded with editor and publisher Pascal Covici the short-lived *Chicago Literary Times*, an absurdist journal of literature and culture.

Much of Hecht's early work, including the plays he wrote with Goodman, coincide with that period of cultural flowering in the city remembered as the Chicago Literary Renaissance. Many cite the founding of Harriet Monroe's *Poetry: A Magazine of Verse* in 1912 as the inauguration of the period, and see it ending with the stock market crash of 1929.[11] Chicago Renaissance writers – Theodore Dreiser, Sherwood Anderson, Carl Sandburg – often shared Hecht's background in journalism. More fully than Goodman and Hecht, these other writers explored themes of "the revolt from the village," the challenges of city life and city labor, and the disintegration of Victorian ideals in the industrialized modern world. Carla Capetti credits the Chicago Renaissance with bringing "the world to Chicago and Chicago to the world".[12] Hecht and Goldman's plays were a small and potent part of the Renaissance.

Hecht had a number of significant collaborations aside from Goodman. With Maxwell Bodenheim, a poet, hobo and satirist, whom he met in the *Poetry* offices in 1912, he wrote, among other titles, *Cutie: A Warm Mama* (1924). With Charles McArthur, journalist and Algonquin roundtable regular, Hecht collaborated intermittently for eighteen years, their most famous work being *The Front Page*, about Chicago reporters covering the Cook County criminal court. The collaboration with Goodman occurred intermittently between 1914 and 1917, with the two writers often working in the elder Goodman's corporation boardroom. Together, Goodman and Hecht wrote about a dozen plays, which Hecht later described as "sane and practical little one-acts".[13]

In 1918, Hecht spent a year in Germany, working as a correspondent for *The Daily News*. In 1926, he moved to Hollywood to get rich in the growing motion picture industry. One of his best-known screenplays is *Scarface* (1932), remade in the 1980s and generating many lines that would become part of the American vernacular. For his 1927 *Underworld* Hecht won an Oscar for best original story; the gold statue remains with Hecht's papers at the Newberry Library. In the final decades of his life Hecht traveled regularly between Hollywood and New York City, where he died in 1964.

The Little Theater Movement

The American Little Theater Movement coincided with and became one aspect of the Chicago Literary Renaissance of the early twentieth century. As early as 1901, Jane Addams's Hull House began producing plays that dealt with the social problems of the South Side's local immigrant populations.[14] Between 1912 and 1916 sixty-three little theaters opened in the U.S.; by 1926, there were five thousand, and Chicago remained the center of the movement. Some theaters attracted working-class, immigrant audiences, while many others drew audience, cast, and financial support from city elites. For this reason some scholars of American theater history claim the Little Theater movement was "essentially – despite populist roots – an elitist enterprise".[15]

Playbill for "The Wonder Hat," Chicago Little Theater, May 19, 1916.
Photo courtesy The Newberry Library, Chicago
(Call no. MMS Goodman, Box 8, Folder 341).

The Little Theaters generally produced short plays
of one or two acts, and had a willingness to experiment
with avant-garde staging techniques. The shows were
usually produced in small venues that seated fewer than
a hundred playgoers; audiences differed in demographics
from theater to theater. Proponents of the Little Theater
Movement objected to the increasingly standardized and
commercial character of theater in the United States.
Maurice Browne, a notable promoter of the movement
who founded the Chicago Little Theater, believed, with
some justification, that a cabal of Broadway producers
controlled play selection and production style for
theaters all over America. Browne felt they chose "the
lowest common denominators in playwriting – obvious
themes, cheap sentiment, childish musical comedy, and
conventional scenery".[16] Little Theater proponents also
opposed what they considered to be the vulgarity and
commercialism of the early motion picture industry.
Constance D'Arcy Mackay, a playwright and director best
remembered for children's theatrical pageants in the
teens and twenties, asserted that the Little Theater was
"the arch-foe of commercialism".[17]

In addition to opposing commercialism, the Little
Theaters also desired to provide a meaningful activity
for the middle class to fill the leisure hours created
by advances in domestic technology. Little Theater
proponents considered commercial productions of the
time to be "intellectually thin, or downright frivolous…
shoddily produced and sometimes falsely advertised…
mindless, bloated, and detrimental to psychic well-
being".[18] In his book *The Civic Theater* (1912),
Percy Mackaye advocated for theater as a means of

"constructive leisure" that would enable playgoers to forge relationships, and improve their communities. Little Theater advocates believed theater could improve American society by offering participants "a chance to explore social issues and to resist the numbing lure of predictably scripted spectacle shows".[19]

Jane Addams founded one of the first Little Theaters in the country in 1901 at Hull House, located at 800 S. Halsted, then a neighborhood of Greek, Italian, and Jewish immigrants. As Constance Mackay put it in a period manifesto for the Little Theaters, the productions staged at Hull House were "interpretive of struggle, of the knowledge of bitter inequalities, of valiant aspirations".[20] Under the direction of Laura Dainty Pelham, an actor and women's suffrage leader, the theater at Hull House drew its casts from the surrounding neighborhoods, often with a handful of uptowners included. In 1917, the theater could seat 230 people. Viola Spolin, whose *Theater Games* would become a classic text in Chicago's improvisational performance community, taught theater classes at Hull House in the 1930s.

Maurice Browne, a British import, founded the Little Theater of Chicago in 1911, describing it as "a repertory and experimental art theater producing classic and modern plays, both tragedy and comedy, at popular prices".[21] Browne produced classical plays like *The Trojan Women* and *Medea*, as well contemporary works like Wilde's *The Happy Prince*, Yeats's *The Shadowy Waters*, and Goodman and Hecht's "The Wonder Hat." Browne claimed that the theater intended no less than "the creation of a new plastic and rhythmic drama in America," and sought to produce highly wrought productions of plays that would not be found in the commercial theaters of the day.[22] Browne's work faced a number of significant challenges including, according to Mackay, "the early prejudice that labeled a Little Theater, 'Dangerous! Beware of Highbrowism'".[23] The theater was located on the 4th floor of the Fine Arts building on Michigan Ave, had a seating capacity of ninety-one, and enjoyed a subscriber membership of four-hundred by 1917.

Also in 1911, Mr. and Mrs. Arthur Aldis established the Playhouse of Lake Forest, in a house next to their home. With a seating capacity of one-hundred, this was a grand suburban house turned into a theater. There was no subscription, admission to events being by invitation only. The Aldis's prided themselves on producing new or challenging material, mostly one-act plays. Since the stage was small, they preferred "static" plays, in which the action was more mental than physical. Produced plays include "Extreme Unction" by Mrs. Aldis, "The Village" by Octave Feuillet, and "Pierrot of the Minute" by Arthur Dowson.[24]

Established in Manhattan in 1915, the Washington Square Players earned a reputation as "the most interesting group of little theater players" in the U.S.[25] The Players' specialized in the development of new work, generally one-act dramas by American playwrights. Much of this material — "Eugenically Speaking" by Edward Goodman, "Two Blind Beggars and One Less Blind" by Philip Moeller, and "The Clod" by Lewis Beach – has not stood the test of time.

The Workshop Theater of Chicago opened in 1916, and by 1917 it had one-hundred active members, one-hundred associated members, and a seating capacity of

Advertisement of one-act plays by the Washington Square
Players, including Goodman's "The Hero of Santa Maria."
Photo courtesy The Newberry Library, Chicago (Call no. MMS
Goodman, Box 7, Folder 326).

eighty. According to its policy, this theater debuted new
work, often one-acts and pantomimes, written by Chicago
authors, acted by Chicago actors, with sets designed
by Chicago artists. The Workshop premiered several of
Kenneth Sawyer Goodman and Ben Hecht's collaborations,
including "The Wonder Hat," "An Idyll of the Shops," and
"The Home Coming." Though the Workshop was the first
to showcase these plays, other theaters nationally would
remount them in subsequent years.

The Arts and Crafts Theater of Detroit, founded in
November 1916, aimed for "the training of true craftsmen,
the developing of individual character in connection with
artistic work, and the raising of standards of beauty".[26]
Entirely financed by the Detroit Arts and Crafts Society,
it was the only Little Theater in the U.S. that worked in
partnership with an art guild. They focused on producing
revivals of old plays of literary significance, such as plays
by Moliere, Corneille, and Marlowe, among others. It
had a seating capacity of two hundred and fifty, and the
company was entirely amateur, albeit selective.

The Players' Club of the Chicago Hebrew Institute
held productions at 1258 West Taylor Street, producing
Goodman's "Back of the Yards" in 1917. The Institute
had been organized in 1903 as a settlement house to
promote the assimilation into mainstream American
society of Eastern-European Jewish immigrants to the
west-side neighborhood. To this end, the Institute offered
classes in citizenship, English, commerce, and literature.
Longtime director Philip L. Seaman described the institute
as "frankly Jewish and staunchly American".[27] In 1922, it
changed its name to The Jewish People's Institute.

Goodman's ubiquity in the Chicago Little Theater

Program for The Players' Workshop, 1916, including Goodman and Hecht's "An Idyll of Shops." Photo courtesy The Newberry Library, Chicago (Call no. MMS Goodman, Box 7, Folder 330).

The Players' Club of the Chicago Hebrew Institute presents "Back of the Yards," 1915. Photo courtesy The Newberry Library, Chicago (Call no. MMS Goodman, Box 7, Folder 316).

scene – as playwright, financial backer, and promoter of dialogue and connections in the city's artistic community – illustrates one aspect of the elitist basis on which the theater's populist project relied, and the alliance between the theaters and the settlement house suggests another. The language of Goodman's plays – sometimes folksy, sometimes mannered – might make Goodman's theater seem old-fashioned to today's audiences. The interconnection of elite and populist elements in Goodman's Little Theater Movement, however, should be familiar to theater-goers, at least in Chicago today, where that interconnection is still very much in force. Whether one attends the "urban interventions" of late and lamented Redmoon theater, or any of the "gritty" and "visceral" productions of Sanford Meisner's many Chicago disciples, or the bio-play of an R&B icon at Jackie Taylor's Black Ensemble Theater, the play, however populist its project, is likely to have been produced through elite or corporate sponsorship.

Commedia dell'Arte

Commedia dell'arte means "professional comedy." The popularity of this tradition in the theater reached its climax in Italy in the sixteenth and seventeenth centuries. Most *commedia dell' arte* plays mixed oral tradition and written culture, as the actors improvised dialogue based on a textual synopsis of the scenes. Plots were often inspired by the prestigious scripted comedy of the day, known as "*commedia erudita*." In a typical plot, the old men (Pantalone and the Doctor) make plans that cannot be realized due to the interference of a pair of young lovers and associated servants and clowns. A mixture of trickery and the discovery of a long-lost family connection would often bring the resolution and end the play.

Characters

Commedia dell'arte promoted virtuoso solo and ensemble performances in ways that more scripted theater did not allow. Actors became highly skilled in playing a certain character or "mask," which they played over a lifetime. *Commedia* performers worked together in troupes which required good chemistry, as each actor had to respond to the other actors' improvisations. Sometimes the troupes were composed of family members for whom acting was the family business. Actors memorized repertoire for the character they would play, and then insert bits, as appropriate in different scenes and contexts. The tradition developed at least eight stock *Commedia dell' arte* characters, which have distinct characteristics, masks, shapes, emotions and even dialects. These characters were meant to be exaggerated portrayals of familiar social types.

Harlequin is a valet from Bergamo. He is usually stupid but occasionally displays some wit. His character is child-like, and he often runs into difficulties. He is clumsy, greedy, credulous, yet charming. Harlequin is usually played by a talented acrobat.

Brighella is a cruel jack-of-all-trades from Bergamo. He is cunning and sharp, always seeking his own pleasure, and for this reason disliked and feared.

Pantalone is a retired merchant from Venice. Greedy and miserly, he has faced financial losses and is frequently duped.

The Doctor is a well-educated Bolognese. A pedant

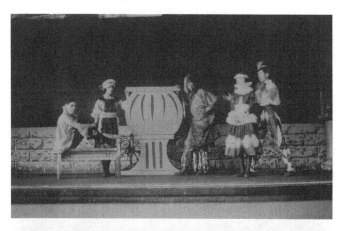

Production images from "The Wonder Hat," Central High
School, Aberdeen, South Dakota. Photo courtesy The Newberry
Library, Chicago (Call no. MMS Goodman, Box 8, Folder 356).

and wind-bag, he knows everything but understands nothing. One of his trademarks is to misquote Latin. He is miserly, conceited, and trivial. Like his friend Pantalone, he is despised and ridiculed by everyone.

Pulcinella is an old bachelor from Benevento. He usually embraces an epicurean way of living, and is gluttonous and selfish. Cruel and witty, Pulcinella was sometimes played as humpbacked.

The Captain is a loud-mouthed military officer, usually from Spain. He tells stories of his great courage but is usually the first to run in a dangerous situation.

Pedrolino (Pierrot) is a sweet-natured and trustworthy valet. Young, sensitive and personable, he is usually the scapegoat and is the one who gets blamed for trickery, though he only had a minor part in it. He sometimes even accepts fault for wrongs he did not commit.

The lovers' primary trait is to be in love. They are usually young and from the court. Their speech is usually elegant and shows their upper-class status. They are courteous and gallant.

Lazzi

Another feature of *commedia dell'arte* are the interludes, known as the *lazzi*, meaning "turn" or "trick," which were sometimes brought into British drama as "Italian business." These were typically the only scripted pieces of the act and, as comic relief, rarely had much to do with the plot. Some actors or troupes became well-known for a certain act and the audience would come to expect it. The *lazzi* could be anything from an acrobatic act to the actors engaging in silly horseplay.

In one way, the Little Theater Movement, along with Goodman's imagination, drew from the classicism of European drama; in another, though, both Goodman

The Wonder Hat

by

BEN HECHT and KENNETH SAWYER GOODMAN

SCENE

A park by moonlight

CHARACTERS

Harlequin	Morgan Drake
Pierrot	Harland Gilbert
Punchinello	Fred Stellner
Columbine	Myrna Clark
Margot	Dorothy Mitchell
Director	Miss Lighthall
Costumes	Miss Flemington
Music	Miss James

High School Orchestra

(Presented with permission of the Stage Guild, Chicago.)

HIGH SCHOOL PRINT SHOP

Playbill from a production of "The Wonder Hat" at Central
High School, Aberdeen, South Dakota.
Photo courtesy The Newberry Library, Chicago (Call no. MMS
Goodman, Box 8, Folder 341).

and the Little Theaters were oriented toward the contemporary American social world with all its diversity and mess. "The Wonder Hat" brings these two orientations together through characters who bear the names (comically altered) and stand in the attitudes of *Commedia dell' arte* types, but who speak in an arresting American vernacular. Goodman's "Back of the Yards," too, with its focus on troubled youths on the streets of Chicago's immigrant neighborhoods, hearkens also to the emerging diversity of American society.

From the apparent whimsy of "The Wonder Hat" to the contrasting realism of "Back of the Yards," these two short plays recall that the reformist agenda of the Little Theater movement existed alongside the movement's deceptively simpler goal of providing entertainment and diversion for an increasingly diverse, modern society.

It may be that the moment is not ripe for a full-fledged Kenneth Sawyer Goodman revival in the Chicago theater scene, but it is beyond argument that the Goodman theater has honored the memory and mission of a playwright whose life and work were inextricably linked to this city. This volume makes two of Goodman's richest plays available in a format illustrated by artists Jaime Deare ("The Wonder Hat) and Emily Murman ("Back of the Yards) who, in engagingly disparate styles, have undertaken "to restore old visions and to win the new."

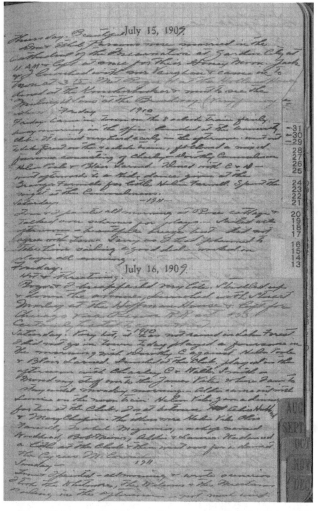

Kenneth Sawyer Goodman's diary entry from July 15th, 1909. Photo courtesy The Newberry Library, Chicago (Call no. MMS Goodman, Box 6, Folder 279).

Endnotes

[1] Our understanding of Goodman and his work with Hecht draws extensively from the Kenneth Sawyer Goodman papers at the Newberry Library. The Newberry's collection of Kenneth Sawyer Goodman's papers includes personal items such as correspondence, drawings, diaries, photographs, and programs from productions of his plays. It also contains artifacts of his literary endeavors, including manuscripts, typescripts and published versions of his solo works and those written in collaboration with Ben Hecht. The collection measures five linear feet and is contained in nine boxes and four scrapbooks. The material collected here offers information about the playwright's childhood, military service, marriage, theatrical works, and death. Goodman subscribed to The Author's Clipping Bureau, and saved notices and reviews about productions of his plays across the country. He painstakingly curated his own work, and evidently remained very interested in the response it provoked. The Newberry inherited from the playwright a collection of papers that is both orderly and nearly exhaustive.

[2] Stuart J. Hecht, "Kenneth Sawyer Goodman: Bridging Chicago's Affluent and Artistic Networks," Theater History Studies 13 (1993): 136.

[3] Hecht, 143.

[4] Ibid.

[5] Jack Hrkach, "Kenneth Sawyer Goodman," in American National Biography (New York: Oxford University Press, 1999), 247.

[6] Hecht, 142.

7 Hrkach, 247.

8 Jeffrey Brown Martin, "Ben Hecht," in American National Biography, Vol. 10. (New York: Oxford University Press, 1999), 481.

9 George Fetherling, The Five Lives of Ben Hecht (Toronto: Lester and Orpen, 1977), 29.

10 Fetherling, 53.

11 Fetherling, 47.

12 Carlo Rotella, "Chicago Literary Renaissance," in The Encyclopedia of Chicago (Chicago: University of Chicago Press, 2004), 140.

13 Fetherling, 23.

14 Constance D'Arcy Mackay, The Little Theater in the United States (New York: Henry Holt, 1917), 115.

15 Jan Pinkerton and Randolph H. Hudson, Encyclopedia of the Chicago Literary Renaissance (New York: Facts On File, 2004), 204.

16 Dennis Kennedy, editor, "Little Theater Movement," in The Oxford Encyclopedia of Theater and Performance, Vol. 1 (New York, NY: Oxford University Press, 2003), 751.

17 Mackay, 1.

18 Dorothy Chansky, Composing Ourselves: The Little Theater Movement and the American Audience (Carbondale: Southern Illinois University Press, 2004), 4).

19 Chansky, 4.

20 Mackay, 115.

[21] Mackay, 103.

[22] Mackay, 104.

[23] Mackay, 104.

[24] Mackay, 124.

[25] Mackay, 29.

[26] Mackay, 147.

[27] Linda J. Borish, "Chicago Hebrew Institute," in The Encyclopedia of Chicago (Chicago: University of Chicago Press, 2004), 135.

Works Cited and Consulted

Bordman, Gerald, and Thomas S. Hischak. "Little Theater in America." *The Oxford Companion to American Theater*. New York: Oxford University Press, 2004. 393-94.

Borish, Linda J. "Chicago Hebrew Institute." *The Encyclopedia of Chicago*. Chicago: University of Chicago Press, 2004. 135.

Chansky, Dorothy. *Composing Ourselves: The Little Theater Movement and the American Audience*. Carbondale: Southern Illinois University Press, 2004.

"Chicago Literary Renaissance." *The Encyclopedia Britannica*. New York: Black Dog & Leventhal, 2008.

"Cupid in Chicago." *Town and Country* [Chicago] 16 Mar. 1912.

Duchartre, Pierre-Louis. *The Italian Comedy: The Improvisation, Scenarios, Lives, Attributes, Portraits, and Masks of the Illustrious Characters of the Commedia Dell'Arte*. Trans. Randolph T. Weaver. New York: Dover Publications, 1966.

Fetherling, George. *The Five Lives of Ben Hecht*. Toronto: Lester and Orpen, 1977.

Hecht, Stuart J. "Kenneth Sawyer Goodman: Bridging Chicago's Affluent and Artistic Networks." *Theater History Studies* 13 (1993): 135-47.

Hrkach, Jack. "Kenneth Sawyer Goodman." *American National Biography*. New York: Oxford University Press, 1999. 246-47.

"Kenneth Sawyer Goodman." Bulletin of the Art Institute of Chicago (1907-1951) 19, no. 6 (1925): 66. http://www.jstor.org/stable/4116890.

Kennedy, Dennis, ed. "Commedia Dell'Arte." *The Oxford Encyclopedia of Theater and Performance*. Vol. 1. New York, NY: Oxford University, 2003. 298-301.

Kennedy, Dennis, ed. "Little Theater Movement." *The Oxford Encyclopedia of Theater and Performance*. Vol. 1. New York, NY: Oxford University, 2003. 751.

Martin, Jeffrey Brown. "Ben Hecht." *American National Biography*. Vol. 10. New York: Oxford University Press, 1999. 481-83.

Mackay, Constance D'Arcy. *The Little Theater in the United States*. New York: Henry Holt, 1917.

MacKaye, Percy. *The Civic Theater in Relation to the Redemption of Leisure*. New York: M. Kennerly, 1912.

McNaughton, Howard. "Ben Hecht." *Playwrights*. Detroit: Gale Research International. 1994. 459–462.

Pinkerton, Jan, and Randolph H. Hudson. *Encyclopedia of the Chicago Literary Renaissance*. New York: Facts On File, 2004.

Rotella, Carlo, "Chicago Literary Renaissance." *The Encyclopedia of Chicago*. Chicago: University of Chicago, 2004. 140.

Smith, Winifred. *The Commedia Dell'Arte: A Study in Italian Popular Comedy*. New York: Columbia University Press, 1912.

THE WONDER HAT

By: Kenneth Sawyer Goodman and Ben Hecht

CHARACTERS

HARLEQUIN
PIERROT
PUNCHINELLO
COLUMBINE
MARGOT

Illustrations by Jaime Deare

"The Wonder Hat" was originally produced at the Arts and Crafts Theatre, Detroit, Michigan, in 1916.

Set designed by Sam Hume

NOTICE: The text of "The Wonder Hat" as given in this edition represents the final revision of the play by the authors.

The Scene is a park by moonlight. The stage setting is shallow. At the back center is a formal fountain, backed by a short wall about seven feet high with urns at its two ends. At each side of the fountain, low groups of shrubbery. There is a clear space between the fountain and the back drop so that the characters may pass around the shrubbery and the fountain. The back drop represents a night sky with an abnormally large and yellow moon. A path crosses the stage parallel to the footlights.

As the curtain rises, HARLEQUIN *and* PIERROT *saunter in from the left, arm in arm. They both have on long cloaks and are swinging light canes with an air of elegant ennui. They pause in the center of the stage.*

HARLEQUIN.   [*Indicating with a wave of his cane*]   Dear fellow, this is a circular path. It runs quite around the outer edge of the park. It delights me. I always spend my evenings here. One can walk for hours with the absolute certainty of never getting anywhere.

PIERROT.   [*Removing his eyeglass*]   Dear chap, in these days of suburban progress, I had not supposed such a place possible.

HARLEQUIN.   Also you may have noticed, all the promenaders move continuously in thwe same direction. It is, therefore, only necessary to maintain an even pace in order to avoid making acquaintances.

PIERROT.   [*With a slight yawn*]   One might retrace one's steps?

HARLEQUIN.   It has been tried by certain elderly roués and ladies from the opera, but always with disastrous results. Our best people no longer attempt it.

PIERROT.   Tell me, does Columbine ever come here?

HARLEQUIN.   [*Becoming serious*]   That is the one drawback. She comes here very often.

PIERROT.   [*Snappishly*]   Humph! That really is annoying, deucedly, devilishly, foolishly annoying!

HARLEQUIN.   You're very emphatic.

PIERROT.   [*Still more snappishly*]   I have never liked that woman, in spite of what the poets say about us.

HARLEQUIN.   By keeping a sharp lookout, I have thus far managed to avoid her myself.

PIERROT.   [*Pleased*]   I see that we are both confirmed bachelors. We agree perfectly.

HARLEQUIN.   On the contrary, we don't agree at all. Because you dislike Columbine, you're too confounded polite to others. You make cynical love to all sorts of women, and nobody likes you for it. On the other hand, I adore her and make love to nobody at all. For that reason, I am simply overwhelmed with dinner invitations.

PIERROT.   Then why don't you catch up with her some evening and tell her so?

HARLEQUIN.   [*Preening himself*]   Gross materialist! She would certainly fall in love with me.

PIERROT.   [*With equal self-satisfaction*]   At least I should be spared the possibility of her falling in love with me.

HARLEQUIN.   How selfish of you! But come, if you are quite rested, let us continue our walk.

We agree perfectly!

PIERROT.   To be perfectly frank, dear chap, I find myself extremely sleepy.

HARLEQUIN.   [*Haughtily*]   There is a beautiful stone bench just beyond that clump of lilacs.

PIERROT.   Thanks. When we reach it, I shall sit down.

HARLEQUIN.   By all means, dear fellow. I can then resume my stroll without the effort of conservation.

> [*They saunter off, arm in arm, toward the right. PUNCHINELLO enters, dressed in a long, ragged, green coat, and carrying a large sack and a little bell. He wears long whiskers and a pair of horn-rimmed spectacles. He advances, tapping before him with a staff and ringing his little bell.*]

PUNCHINELLO.   [*In a whining sing-song*]   New loves for old! New loves for old! I will buy broken ambitions, wasted lives, cork legs, rejected poems, unfinished plays, bottles, bootjacks, and worn-out religions. [*He drops his pack.*] Oyez! Oyez! Oyez! New loves for old! New loves for old! [*He wags his head, listening.*] Nobody here. I've walked three times 'round this accursed park. I've seen moon-faced boys asleep on stone benches, stone Tritons blowing water into the air, and a rabble of sick-looking poets and silly-looking girls all walking in the same direction. But not one bona-fide customer! I'll sit down. Yes, yes, I'll sit down, curse them, and ease this infernal crick in my back.

> [*He unfolds a little camp stool which he carries, slung by a strap, and sits down. COLUMBINE*]

and MARGOT *enter from the left and advance timidly to the center of the stage without noticing* PUNCHINELLO.]

COLUMBINE.   [*Very much* excited]   I'm sure, Margot, that I saw him here only a moment ago.

MARGOT.   Do you wait my honest opinion, Mistress Columbine?

COLUMBINE.   [*Stamping her foot*]   How can an opinion be anything but honest? An opinion is naturally and automatically honest.

MARGOT.   Mine ain't, ma'am. I always formulates my opinions to conform.

COLUMBINE.   I don't want them. I'm miserable. I'm wretched.

MARGOT.   [*Severely*]   Then I won't give them to you. But if you'd act more like a lady and stop trapesing around in the damp of the night trying to scrape acquaintance with — with this Harlequin, who, God knows, may have six or seven wives already—

COLUMBINE.   I'm not trapesing after him!

PUNCHINELLO.   [*In his sing-song voice*]   New loves for old! New loves for old!

COLUMBINE.   [*Frightened*]   Oh, how you startled me!

PUNCHINELLO.   [*Rubbing his hands*]   Bargains, cheap, wonderful bargains. What will the lady buy? Something for her parlor? Something for her bedroom? Something for herself? Wall paper, egg beaters, canary birds, salt shakers, oriental rugs, corset covers, diamonds, water

bags, churns, potato peelers, hats, shoes, gas fixtures,
new—old — bargains, lady, bargains?

COLUMBINE.   No, no, no! I don't want to buy anything.

PUNCHINELLO.   [*Kneeling and spreading out his wares*]
I have cures to sell, and charms.

COLUMBINE.   [*Fascinated in spite of herself*]   What —
what charms have you?

PUNCHINELLO.   Ho, ho! I have a charm to ward off evil
spirits.

MARGOT.   [*In disgust*]   Get along with you!

PUNCHINELLO.   Ha, ha! Against nightmares, then;
against mice, toothaches, bunions, burglars, and broken
legs.

COLUMBINE.   I don't want them—any of them.

PUNCHINELLO.   [*Wagging his head*]   Ho, ho! Ha, ha!
Then you're in love. You want a love charm.

COLUMBINE.   [*Stamping her foot*]   You're impudent! I
tell you I'm not in love.

MARGOT.   [*Beginning to be interested*]   What makes
you pipe her off as being in love?

PUNCHINELLO.   A lady who isn't interested in mice,
bunions, or burglars must be in love. There's no two
ways about it.

MARGOT.   What about the broken legs and toothaches?

PUNCHINELLO.   [*Spreading his hands*]   I just put that in
for good measure.

I tell you I'm <u>not</u> in love.

COLUMBINE.   Enough! I won't listen to you; I—I'm not in love.

PUNCHINELLO.   I can remedy that with a charm.

COLUMBINE.   [*Almost in tears*]   I don't want your charms. I don't want to be in love. I hate him! I hate him! I hate him! So there!

PUNCHINELLO.   Yes, yes, pretty lady. I know that sort of talk very well. But I have also a charm to attract love.

COLUMBINE.   [*Brightening immediately*]   You have a charm to attract love?

PUNCHINELLO.   It will bring all men to you; little men, big men, pretty men, noble men, fat men —

COLUMBINE.   [*Clasping her hands*]   I want only one man — only Harlequin.

MARGOT.   [*Interrupting*]   If you want my opinion, ma'am —

COLUMBINE.   But I don't. I want the charm.

MARGOT.   I'd leave this fellow's stuff alone, if I was you.

COLUMBINE.   But you're not me. I want the charm.

PUNCHINELLO.   [*Searching through his wares*]   It will bring Harlequin to you with the rest.

COLUMBINE.   [*On tiptoe with eagerness*]   Quick! Give it to me.

PUNCHINELLO.   [*Taking an old slipper from his pocket*]   Ho, ho! Here it is. An old slipper! Each stitch of it more effective than Sappho's complete works. Each thread more potent than the burning caresses of Dido. They say Cinderella wore a crystal slipper. It's a lie. This — this is what she wore. Ah, ha! Look at it!

COLUMBINE.   [*Taken aback*]   Do I have to wear that?

MARGOT.   [*Scornfully*]   Land's sake, it's all run down at the heel.

PUNCHINELLO.   That's because it has been worn so often. Semiramis of Babylon, Laïs of Corinth, and Thaïs of Alexandria, all wore this boot.

MARGOT.   [*With a sniff*]   Them names don't sound like respectable ladies, to my way of thinking.

COLUMBINE.   [*Dubiously*]   It looks very old. Are you sure it has been fumigated?

PUNCHINELLO.   It's no older than the light it will kindle in a thousand eyes when you wear it. But in its antiquity lies its chief charm. Cleopatra of Egypt abetted the lures of her person with this same ragged boot. Mary of Scotland and a hundred other beauties of history have inspired the enraptured supplications of their adorers with no more tangible asset then this homely boot. Put it on, pretty lady, and all the men will flock to your feet, especially to the foot that wears the slipper.

[*He hands* COLUMBINE *the slipper*]

COLUMBINE.   Ooh, ooh! How wonderful!

MARGOT.   [*With a superior air*]   Take my word, miss, it'll be a nuisance to you.

COLUMBINE.   I don't care. I'm going to teach Harlequin a lesson he won't forget.

Oh, most wonderful lady!

[*She takes off her own shoe, hopping on one foot
and holding* MARGOT'S *arm. She then puts on
the magic slipper.*]

MARGOT.   Mind, I warned you now.

COLUMBINE.   [*Stamping her foot down*]   There! It
doesn't look so badly once I get it on.

PUNCHINELLO.   [*Groveling on his knees, his hands
clasped*]   Oh, most wonderful lady! Oh, most beautiful,
most gracious, most divine lady!

MARGOT.   [*Amazed at* PUNCHINELLO'S *sudden fervor*]
Lord love us! What's got into the old bag of bones?

PUNCHINELLO.   [*To* COLUMBINE]   You have melted the
lump of ice in my old breast. I am young again. I can hear
the birds singing, and sweet waters falling.

MARGOT.   [*To* PUNCHINELLO]   Get up this minute,
before I burst a lung bawling for help.

COLUMBINE.   [*Dancing up and down with delight*]   Oh,
oh, oh! Now I know it works!

MARGOT.   Just the same, he ought to know better, the
old grumpus.

PUNCHINELLO.   I love you.

COLUMBINE.   [*Gently*]   That's very nice in you, of
course, but please get up, and tell me how much I owe
you.

PUNCHINELLO.   [*Still on his knees*]   With all my heart,
with all my soul!

MARGOT.   Don't you hear her? How much does she owe
you for the magic slipper?

PUNCHINELLO. [*Still groveling*]   Nothing! Nothing! You owe me nothing at all! I will give you everything in my sack, all my bargains, all my spells, all my charms. I will make you a witch.

MARGOT.   She don't want to be a witch. She wouldn't touch them with the tip of a barge pole.

COLUMBINE. [*To* MARGOT]   I really think I ought to pay him.

MARGOT.   If he won't take anything, he won't. That's all there is to it.

PUNCHINELLO.   Speak to me! My heart is bursting.

MARGOT.   Let it burst then. Come, ma'am.

COLUMBINE.   Yes, yes. Let's run.

> [COLUMBINE *takes* MARGOT *by the hand and they run off to the right, laughing.*]

PUNCHINELLO. [*Attempting to rise*]   Wait! Wait! I — I — Oh, confound this stitch in my side! [*As the girls' voices die away he struggles to his feet and rubs his head in a dazed sort of way.*] Gone! What have I done? By the seven witches of Beelzebub, by the long-fanged mother of the Great Green Spider, I've been tricked, cheated. [*He shakes his staff.*] Curses on her golden head! May she have nightmares and toothache. May — Old fool! A blight on my whiskers! Woe! Woe! I've given my darling slipper away for nothing.

> [*He sits down again on his camp stool and rocks to and fro, muttering.* HARLEQUIN, *having completed his circle of the park, enters from the left. He is smoking a cigarette and*

strolls along wearing a gloomy and troubled
expression. PUNCHINELLO *sees him and*
resumes his whining chant.]

PUNCHINELLO.   New loves for old. New loves for old.
Bargains in cast-off sweethearts, old coats, umbrellas,
glove buttoners, and household pets. Bargains sir,
bargains! Cheap, wonderful bargains! [HARLEQUIN *passes*
and regards PUNCHINELLO *with absolute indifference.*]
I have pipes, swords, hosiery, snuff boxes, underwear,
wines, trinkets for beautiful ladies, furniture, spy glasses,
motor cars, and bottle openers.

HARLEQUIN.   [*Impatiently*]   I want none of your
bargains.

PUNCHINELLO.   I have magic bargains, sir. Spells and
charms.

HARLEQUIN.   Ah! More like it! You have charms, eh?
What kind of charms?

PUNCHINELLO.   I have charms against bunions,
burglars, broken legs, nightmares, stomachaches, and
hangnails.

HARLEQUIN.   Ordinary trash! I don't want them.

PUNCHINELLO.   [*Looking furtively about*]   I have a love
charm.

HARLEQUIN.   [*In alarm*]   God forbid!

PUNCHINELLO.   [*Rubbing his hands*]   Ho, ho! He, he!

HARLEQUIN.   Have you, by any chance, a charm against
love? ye, more, have you some efficacious armor against
womankind in general?

PUNCHINELLO.   Ho, ho! A man after my own heart, a cautious man. A sensible man.

HARLEQUIN.   [*Loftily*]   Know you, antiquated pander, that everywhere I go, women follow me. They stalk me. They covet me. They make my days miserable. They haunt my sleep. They simper about me, wink at me; rub against me like silken cats. [*With vexation.*] Ah, I would almost end my life from very irritation. And the damnable part of it is that I know myself susceptible.

PUNCHINELLO.   [*Slyly*]   There is no charm in the world against falling in love, but I can sell you a powder, which, tossed into the air, will bring destruction to women alone.

HARLEQUIN.   [*Rubbing his chin doubtfully*]   No, that's too brutal. I couldn't kill them all even if I wanted to. And what use then to destroy a hundred, a thousand, even a million women, and have one sneak up behind you and get you after all. It would be an effort wasted. Love is inevitable.

PUNCHINELLO.   Wait! Ho, ho! I have it, the very thing! If one cannot remove the inevitable, at any rate one can hide from it. What doesn't see you, can't get you. Ha, ha! I can sell you a hat.

HARLEQUIN.   I am not in the market for a hat.

PUNCHINELLO.   [*Triumphantly*]   But, a magic hat! Ho, such a hat! A wonder hat! It will make you invisible.

HARLEQUIN.   [*Incredulously*]   Invisible?

PUNCHINELLO.   [*Fishing in his bag*]   When you put it on, you will exist only in your own mind. You will

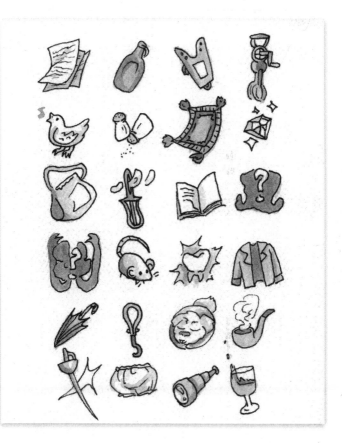

Cheap, wonderful bargains!

escape the pernicious sentimentality, the never-ending blandishments, the strategic coquetry—

HARLEQUIN. [*Eagerly*]   Quick, you millinery sorcerer! You have convinced me. Invisibility is the one thing I crave to make me sublimely happy. Splendid! They shall never simper at me again, never rub against me again, never undulate before my tormented eyes. I will buy it.

PUNCHINELLO. [*Holding up the hat*]   Is it not a creation?

HARLEQUIN. [*Looking at the hat with distaste*]   God, what a thing to wear! I would not wear it, you may be sure, were it not invisible. Any man would prefer not to be seen in such a hat.

PUNCHINELLO.   It may be unlovely in outline, coarse in texture, unrefined in color, but there is only one other such hat in the world. It belongs to the Grand Lama of Thibet. Ha, ha! This one will cost you gold.

HARLEQUIN. [*Cautiously*]   But, first I must see if it is really a wonder hat.

PUNCHINELLO.   I will put it on.

          [*He does so*]

HARLEQUIN. [*Delighted*]   A miracle! Where are you?

PUNCHINELLO. [*Removing the hat with a flourish*] Now!

HARLEQUIN.   What wonders I will do with that hat. But stay! What if the hat is only charmed for you? What if the charm does not apply to me?

PUNCHINELLO.   You shall try it yourself. Put it on.

[HARLEQUIN *takes the hat and puts it on*]

HARLEQUIN.   Can you see me?

PUNCHINELLO.   By St. Peter of Padua, not a speck of you!

> [*He gropes with his hands, then strikes out with his staff and strikes* HARLEQUIN *in the shins.*]

HARLEQUIN.   [*Hopping up and down*]   Ooh! Ouch!

PUNCHINELLO.   Ho, ho! Pardon me. You see you are quite invisible.

HARLEQUIN.   But not invulnerable!

> [*He rubs his shins.*]

PUNCHINELLO.   How much will you give me for this wonder hat?

HARLEQUIN.   Are you sure you can't see me?

PUNCHINELLO.   [*Rubbing his hands*]   You are one with the thin air and the fairies that inhabit it.

HARLEQUIN.   There's no uncanny trick by which Columbine can discover me?

PUNCHINELLO.   None. None. I swear it. It's only by your voice that I know where you are.

PUNCHINELLO.   [*He swings out with his staff.* HARLEQUIN *leaps nimbly aside*]   For years I have treasured this wonder hat. A blind woman with seven teeth and one eye made it in a haunted hut. It was cooked over a fire of

I wonder if I have a
hand or a leg, or a stomach,
or a heart?

serpent skins. [*As* PUNCHINELLO *speaks* HARLEQUIN *tiptoes away to the right around the central group of shrubbery.*] Ho, ho! There's' no charm like it to be had from one peak of the world to the other. [*He swings out again with his staff.* HARLEQUIN, *who has been peeping at him over the shrubbery, disappears behind the fountain.*] Five bags of gold, sir. Cheap—a bargain! Hey! [*He swings his staff.*] Hey! Hey! Where are you? Take off my hat. Give me back my hat! [*He stands still and listens.*] Thief! Thief! He's gone—vanished. Oh, what a fool! First my magic slipper, worth fifty pots of gold. What a doddering idiot! I've been cheated again, robbed, plundered! Oh, what a stitch in my side! Oh, oh! [*He gathers up his pack hurriedly, then stops and taps the side of his nose with his finger.*] Ho, ho! A thought! What a pair of lovers they will make. She with her slipper. He with his hat. She said Harlequin. He said Columbine. Yes, yes! I shall have my reward. They are the fools, not I. As if love were not enough magic of itself. Ho, ho, ho! I must follow her. Ho, ho! She went this way.

> [*He moves off to the right, leaving his camp stool.* HARLEQUIN *appears again around the left end of the shrubbery and advances cautiously to center of the stage.*]

HARLEQUIN. [*Looking after* PUNCHINELLO] I detest the idea of cheating anybody. But of course, one can't be running after trades people, pressing money on them. It simply isn't done. [*He looks in the other direction.*] Columbine should have made the round of the park by this time. What's keeping her? Confound it, here I am waiting for her as safe and invisible as the angels themselves. [*He sits down on the camp stool and holds his hand before his face.*] No, I can't see it. I wonder if I have a hand or a leg, or a stomach, or a heart? If I don't take off my hat and look at myself, I shall soon become a total stranger to myself. What a wonder hat! [*There is a sound of women's voices in the distance. He pricks up his ears.*] Ah, her voice! Like the tinkling of silver bells in a shrine of ivory. Like the patter of crystal rain in a pool of scarlet lilies. [*He slaps his leg.*] Ah, ha! I'm in love! In love, by gad! to the tips of where my fingers ought to be. [*He becomes serious.*] If I take off my hat, I'd be lost. She would pounce on me, and being in love, I should pounce back. My hat must stay on. I will tie it on. I will nail it on. Curse me if I take off my hat. [*He pulls his hat down to the tops of his ears, then clasps his hands.*] Ah, to sit by her, safe and unseen! To bask in the splendor of her presence! To love and be loved only as a dream! To be free from all material entanglements and responsibilities! To touch her with invisible fingers and permit the stolen thrills to course up and down my invisible spine!

[*He sings "Wandering Minstrel Air"*]

> *A love-sick atom I,*
> *A thing unseen and seeing.*
> *For in my hat am I*
> *A hypothetical being.*

[*He suddenly has a new thought.*]

But what if, being unable to see me, she should fall in love with somebody else? That vapid ass, Pierrot, for instance? Oh, God, what if he should strike fire in her heart? But I will not take off my hat! Kind heaven, give me the strength to keep my hat on.

[*He pulls the hat still further over his ears, just as* COLUMBINE *and* MARGOT *enter from the left.*]

COLUMBINE.   This is too much! Did you ever see such a rabble?

MARGOT.   I shouldn't be so particular, miss, seeing as how you brought it on yourself.

COLUMBINE.   They've risen from every bench to follow me. They've come from every corner of the park; burglars, doctors, poets, whiskered Don Juans, rumbling Romeos. Great Heavens, the idiots ! If they hadn't fallen to fighting among themselves, we'd have been trampled to death. I — I hope they exterminate each other.

> [HARLEQUIN, *seeing* COLUMBINE *in such an angry mood, rises cautiously, and in so doing, upsets the camp stool. He stands trembling and holding on to his hat*]

MARGOT.   [*Starting*]   Bless me, what's that?

> [COLUMBINE *and* MARGOT *Both look around. Their eyes pass over* HARLEQUIN *without seeing him*]

COLUMBINE.   Nothing! There's nobody here.

> [*Evidently much relieved,* HARLEQUIN *tiptoes to the right end of the fountain*]

MARGOT.   If you want my honest opinion, miss —

COLUMBINE.   [*Stamping her foot*]   How many times must I tell you —

MARGOT.   Be careful with that magic boot, miss.

COLUMBINE.   Drat the magic boot! What's the good of it? It's brought me nothing but trouble.

MARGOT.   Well, what did you expect?

COLUMBINE.   [*Almost weeping*]   It hasn't brought him. It hasn't brought Harlequin.

MARGOT.   If you want my opinion, miss, honest or otherwise—

COLUMBINE.   [*Stamping her foot again*]   I don't!

MARGOT.   Then I won't give it to you.

COLUMBINE.   Oh, Margot, be gentle with me. I love him, and—and I'm dreadfully uncomfortable about it.

MARGOT.   Well, there's worse discomfort. There's clergyman's sore throat, for instance, and housemaid's knee.

COLUMBINE.   [*Clinching her hands*]   Oh, if I could only see him now, the cold-hearted fish! I'd fix him! I'd melt his icy blood for him!

[HARLEQUIN *holds tight to his hat*]

MARGOT.   [*Soothingly*]   Of course, of course you would.

COLUMBINE.   But he can't escape. I will marry him. I'll marry him. I'll have him for my own, locked under key in a house; a beautiful little house, all new and spick and span, with white trimmings and green shutters.

MARGOT.   If I may put in a word for myself, miss, I hope you won't have a basement kitchen.

COLUMBINE.   [*Spitefully*]   But I'll make him suffer first. I'll — I'll—

[HARLEQUIN *jams his hat down tighter and
    disappears behind the fountain*]

MARGOT.   If you must get het up and stamp, miss, I'd
advise you to confine your stamping to the foot which
ain't got the magic boot on.

COLUMBINE.   Margot, were you ever in love?

MARGOT.   There are opinions concerning that question,
miss, honest and otherwise.

COLUMBINE.   Hush! Some one's coming.

[PIERROT *enters disheveled and breathless. He
    advances and flings himself on one knee before*
    COLUMBINE]

PIERROT.   At last! Exquisite Columbine, ravishing
vision, I have overcome my rivals. I have vanquished a
legion of your adorers.

[HARLEQUIN *peeps round the left side of the
    fountain.*]

MARGOT.   Lord love us! You look as though you'd been
run through a threshing machine.

PIERROT.   I have. I kicked Scaramouche in the stomach
and pushed the Doctor of Bologna into a lily pond. Divine
Circe, I have come to claim my reward.

[*He clutches at the edge of* COLUMBINE'S *dress.*]

COLUMBINE.   Get up this instant! You're tearing the
trimming off my petticoat.

PIERROT.   Columbine, Columbine. I love you!

MARGOT. [*Taking* PIERROT'S *arm and pulling him to his feet*] Get up, you great baby!

> [HARLEQUIN *tiptoes across the stage and stands behind* MARGOT *and* PIERROT.]

PIERROT. [*Clasping his hands*] I love you, Columbine! Listen to me!

COLUMBINE. [*Haughtily*] This is a very sudden change on your part, Mr. Pierrot. Yesterday you snubbed me quite openly.

PIERROT. Forgive me. I was blind I was a dolt. I have only just now come to my senses.

MARGOT. [*Turning her shoulder to him and folding her arms*] You'll come to something worse presently.

PIERROT. [*To* COLUMBINE] I love you—I love you—

> [HARLEQUIN *reaches out and deftly extracts a long hat pin from the back of* MARGOT'S *cap.* MARGOT *puts her hands to her head and turns fiercely on* PIERROT]

MARGOT. How dast you grab my hat?

PIERROT. [*In astonishment*] I never touched your hat.

MARGOT. You did.

PIERROT. [*Turning on her*] I — I did nothing of the sort.

MARGOT. There's laws to cover this kind of thing — annoying women in a public park.

PIERROT. You're an impudent hussy.

Get up, you great baby!

MARGOT.   You're nothing but a common, ordinary home wrecker.

> [HARLEQUIN *approaches* COLUMBINE *and gently touches her hair.* PIERROT *and* MARGOT *glare at each other*]

COLUMBINE.   [*Clasping her hands*]   Margot, Margot, it's wonderful! It's divine! I feel as if the air were suddenly full of kisses.

> [HARLEQUIN *strikes an attitude of complete satisfaction.*]

MARGOT.   It's full of dampness and nasty language, that's what it is.

> [*She gives* PIERROT *a venomous look.*]

PIERROT.   [*Again falling on his knees and addressing* COLUMBINE]   It's full of unspeakable ecstasy of my adoration.

COLUMBINE.   [*Paying no attention to* PIERROT]   It's full of marvelously shy caresses! They are like the wings of happy butterflies, brushing the white lilac blooms.

PIERROT.   Ah, what did I tell you? The love I offer you is a gift, a treasure.

COLUMBINE.   [*Her hands still clasped*]   I can almost feel invisible lips sighing my name — his lips — Harlequin's lips.

PIERROT.   [*Straightening up on his knees*]   What's that you say about Harlequin?

COLUMBINE.   It's none of your business.

PIERROT. [*Spitefully*] Good God! To think of intruding that fellow's name at a time like this. Why, the chap's a positive bounder. He has no taste, no education, no refinement. And his face — ugh! He'd frighten himself to death if he looked in a mirror before his barber got to him in the morning. [HARLEQUIN *steps behind* PIERROT *and prods him in the back with the hat pin.*] Ooh, Ouch! [*He springs to his feet and turns on* MARGOT, *shaking his finger in her face.*] You — you did that. You — you know you did.

MARGOT. [*Taken aback*] Did what?

PIERROT. [*In a rage*] You — you stabbed me in the back and don't you deny it.

MARGOT. The man's stark, staring mad!

COLUMBINE. [*To* PIERROT *in an icy voice*] Will you be good enough to explain what's the matter with you?

PIERROT. [*His eye still on* MARGOT] I've been attacked, lacerated.

MARGOT. If you don't behave yourself, I'll give you something to howl about.

PIERROT. [*Again falling at* COLUMBINE's *feet*] But it's nothing—nothing to the torments I suffer from your heartlessness. Nothing to the —

[HARLEQUIN *stabs him again with the hat pin.*]

PIERROT. Ouch! Wow! Hell's fire! Animals! [*He claps his hand to the spot*] I'm being bitten to death!

MARGOT. And a good riddance, too!

COLUMBINE.   Come, Margot. I won't stay here! I won't be insulted!

PIERROT.   [*Again grasping the hem of her dress*]   No, no! I'll suffer everything. I'll suffer in silence. Only don't leave me. Speak to me. I love you. I—

COLUMBINE.   I'll scream for help.

MARGOT.   If you really want help, miss, it's my advice, take off the slipper.

> [HARLEQUIN, *who has been about to attack*
> PIERROT, *hesitates and looks puzzled.*]

COLUMBINE.   Yes, yes. Why didn't I think of it?

> [*She whips off the magic slipper and holds it in
> her hand. The moment the slipper leaves her
> foot* PIERROT *sits back on his haunches and lets
> go of the edge of* COLUMBINE'S *dress.*]

PIERROT.   [*In a feeble voice*]   I love you. I— [*He rubs his head.*] By Jove, this is most extraordinary!

MARGOT.   [*Clapping her hands*]   Toss it to me, miss.

> [COLUMBINE *tosses the slipper to* MARGOT.]

MARGOT.   [*Examining the slipper*]   What a rummy slipper! [*She takes off her shoe.*] I wonder what's inside of it? Love? [*She puts it on her own foot*] Ooh! How it tickles!

> [PIERROT *rises from his knees and looks
> helplessly from* COLUMBINE *to* MARGOT]

COLUMBINE.   Well, Mr. Pierrot?

What's that you say
about Harlequin?

PIERROT.   [*Completely puzzled*]   I am quite at a loss to explain my feelings.

> [*He hesitates, then turns and kneels before* MARGOT. HARLEQUIN *appears even more puzzled. He is also drawn toward* MARGOT *by the spell of the slipper, but his natural infatuation for* COLUMBINE *seems to neutralize the charm. He is visibly perplexed.*]

PIERROT.   Incomparable Margot! Queen among housemaids! Divine custodian of my deepest affection.

MARGOT.   [*To* COLUMBINE]   You see, miss, the gentleman is now in love with me.

COLUMBINE.   Disgusting!

PIERROT.   I am drawn by some irresistible power of fascination. I—I belong to you utterly.

MARGOT.   You belong in jail. You're nothing but a—a shameless affinity.

PIERROT.   [*Clinging to the hem of* MARGOT'S *skirt*]   I love you. I swear it.

MARGOT.   [*Weakening*]   Oh, la, la! Listen to the man talk!

COLUMBINE.   [*To* MARGOT]   You're a brazen hussy to take advantage of your social superior.

MARGOT.   [*Haughtily*]   My superior? Him?

COLUMBINE.   [*Stamping her foot*]   You're forgetting your place!

PIERROT.   I love you——I love you——

MARGOT.   [*Slyly*]   Suppose, miss, I was to say I believe every word he says to me.

COLUMBINE.   I'd say you were an artful designing minx. I'd discharge you without a shred of character.

MARGOT.   Well, you won't have to—because, I ain't going to say it.

PIERROT.   [*Making another grab at her skirts*]   You must listen to me! You must! [HARLEQUIN *stabs him once more with the hat pin.*] Ouch! Wow! This is terrible. I love you.

MARGOT.   [*To* PIERROT]   Hey! Get up. A woman what works for a living can't afford to have her good nerves shattered for her.

[*She tries to shake off* PIERROT.]

COLUMBINE.   Give me back the slipper, this instant.

MARGOT.   You're welcome to it, I'm sure. [*She snatches off the slipper and tosses it away from her.* COLUMBINE *picks it up, but does not put it on.*] Now will you leave go of me?

[*He releases her in a dazed way*]

PIERROT.   I—I love you. I—

[*He rises and again looks from one to the other.* COLUMBINE *holds the slipper in her hand.*]

COLUMBINE.   [*to* PIERROT]   Well, sir?

MARGOT.   Well?

PIERROT.   [*Adjusting his collar and speaking quite calmly*]   I consider myself fortunate in having escaped you both. I see now that there is something deadly about that slipper. To think that a man of my intellectual and artistic attainments should have been affected by such a trick. In love with a boot! How very trivial!

MARGOT.   Well, what are you going to do now?

PIERROT.   I don't know exactly. Perhaps I shall drown myself in the fountain.

> [*He turns his back on* MARGOT *and* COLUMBINE *and assumes a pose of thoughtful indifference.* HARLEQUIN *again approaches* COLUMBINE.]

COLUMBINE.   Margot, Margot, what shall I do? I'm faint. I'm intoxicated. He hasn't come and yet I feel as if he were near me, almost touching me. I feel all the exquisite certainty of love. Yes, yes, I love him! I love Harlequin, and I know that he loves me in return. I know it, and yet, and yet —

MARGOT.   Yes, miss, and yet—?

COLUMBINE.   [*Wringing her hands*]   And yet I don't know what under heavens to do about it.

> [HARLEQUIN *clasps his hands in an ecstasy of complete satisfaction.*]

MARGOT.   It's my advice, miss, put the slipper on again. What if it don't attract this here Harlequin? There's just as big perch in the puddle as ever came out of it. That's my motto. Besides, there is such a thing as making the right man jealous.

In love with a boot!

You know very well what I want.

COLUMBINE. [*Brightening immediately*] I believe you're right. I'll put on the slipper. I'll have a desperate flirtation with Pierrot. I'll take him everywhere with me. I'll dangle him before Harlequin's eyes. [*She puts on the slipper and speaks archly*] Mr. Pierrot.

PIERROT. [*Turning*] Eh? I beg your pardon.

COLUMBINE. I—I don't want you to be angry with me.

> [PIERROT *looks puzzled for a moment, then succumbs again to the spell of the slipper and rushes toward her.*]

PIERROT. I—I don't—I— [*He throws himself on his knees*] Columbine! My angel!

COLUMBINE. [*Shaking her finger at him*] You were very rude to me a few moments ago. [HARLEQUIN *watches with puzzled interest.*] You accused me of having ensnared your affections by means of a charm.

PIERROT. I don't know anything about a charm. I am charmed only by your eyes, your lips, the flow of your voice.

COLUMBINE. Do you know, I think it's very sweet of you to say that.

PIERROT. I can say more, a thousand times more.

HARLEQUIN. [*Overcome by jealousy*] I shall put a stop to this. [*He seems to come to a tremendous resolve.*] I—I shall take off my hat.

MARGOT. Lord have mercy! What is that?

PIERROT. My adored Columbine! You love me after all?

COLUMBINE.   [*Archly*]   I haven't said so.

HARLEQUIN.   [*Tugging frantically at his* hat]   My hat! A thousand devils! I can't get it off!

PIERROT.   [*Rising*]   I'm your worshipper, your slave.

COLUMBINE.   You may see me to my door.

[*She takes* PIERROT'S *arm.*]

HARLEQUIN.   [*Frantically*]   Wait! Stop! Confound it, if I could only get my hat off!

MARGOT.   [*Alarmed*]   I want to get away from here.

COLUMBINE.   [*Listening*]   It's Harlequin's voice.

PIERROT.   I don't see anybody.

[*They all look about them.* PUNCHINELLO *enters from the left with his pack on his back.*]

PUNCHINELLO.   Ho, ho! Ha, ha! There you are, eh? There you are. I've been looking for you.

[COLUMBINE *hastily snatches off her slipper and hides it behind her. They all face* PUNCHINELLO. HARLEQUIN *tiptoes to one side and watches curiously*]

COLUMBINE.   [*To* PUNCHINELLO]   What do you want?

PUNCHINELLO.   What do I want, eh? You know very well what I want. I want my magic slipper, my magic slipper that you stole from me.

COLUMBINE.   I didn't steal it. You gave it to me!

PUNCHINELLO.   Ho, ho! That's a pretty story! Hee, hee! I gave it to you, eh? Well, I changed my mind.

COLUMBINE.   I—I'm perfectly willing to pay you for it.

MARGOT.   Don't you give him a cent, the miserable oyster.

COLUMBINE.   How much do you want for it?

PUNCHINELLO.   [*Rubbing his hands*]   I should think about ten bags of gold.

COLUMBINE.   Ridiculous! There isn't so much money in the whole world.

PUNCHINELLO.   [*Pointing to* PIERROT]   Perhaps this nice gentleman would like to buy it for you?

PIERROT.   I— [*He looks at Columbine*]   I have only the most casual acquaintance with this lady.

HARLEQUIN.   [*In a rage, to* PIERROT]   You infernal little cad! You—you—

> [*He makes a move toward* PIERROT. *All back away from his voice but* PUNCHINELLO]

PUNCHINELLO.   Ho, ho! So you're there too. Two birds with one stone. [*He rubs his hands.*] My magic slipper and my beloved wonder hat. Well, well, well! [HARLEQUIN, *seeing that he has betrayed his presence, stands as if undecided what to do next.* PUNCHINELLO *strikes about him with his staff.*] Hey! Where are you? Take off my hat.

MARGOT.   For the love of heaven, what is he raving about now?

PUNCHINELLO.   My hat, my wonder hat. I sold it to him for only five bags of gold — six bags of gold—

COLUMBINE.   You sold it to Harlequin?

PUNCHINELLO.   Aye, the ruffian, the highwayman. I sold it to him for only seven bags of gold. He clapped it on his head and now he's invisible.

COLUMBINE.   [*In delighted wonder*]   You really mean that Harlequin is here, near us? Oh, I knew it! I felt it!

PUNCHINELLO.   Of course, he's here. Hey, you take off my hat! [*He swings his staff and* HARLEQUIN *again dances out of the way*] Take off my hat or give me my eight bags of gold. [*He swings his staff again*] Hey, thief!

HARLEQUIN.   I'm not a thief. I'd have paid you for your hat if you hadn't run away in such a huff. Now, after the way you've acted, I shall take my own time about it.

COLUMBINE.   [*Stamping her foot*]   Harlequin!

HARLEQUIN.   [*In a dubious voice*]   Ye—yes?

COLUMBINE.   Take off that silly hat this minute.

HARLEQUIN.   I—well—to tell the truth, I—

COLUMBINE.   Don't you hear what I'm saying? Give it back this second.

HARLEQUIN.   I would first like some sort of assurance, some guaranty of good faith—some—

COLUMBINE.   I'm not making any promises this evening.

Take that silly hat off
this min<u>u</u>te.

HARLEQUIN. [*Plaintively*]   My dear Columbine, I have learned a good deal about my own feelings in the last half hour. I am perfectly willing to return this man's property and to submit to the ordinary and normal risks of society. But I positively insist that, before I reveal myself, you must also return to him all and sundry charms, spells, et cetera, which might, if used either by accident or with malice aforethought, affect my own future course of action.

COLUMBINE. [*Remaining absolutely firm*]   I've told you once that I won't make any promises.

HARLEQUIN.   Then, I remain invisible.

PUNCHINELLO.   I tell you once more, give me back my hat.

HARLEQUIN. [*Folding his arms*]   No.

PUNCHINELLO.   Ah, ha! Then I shall have my revenge! Know, miserable butterfly, that you are trifling with magic beyond your own powers of control. There is a terrible clause in the incorporation of this hat. Ho, ho! Listen! He who steals this wonder hat and places it upon his own head, cannot remove it again except in the presence and with the consent of its rightful owner. When I have left you, you will become for all time one with the interstellar atoms. You will never resume your mortal shape. You will haunt the cafés. You will moon about the boxes at the opera. You will sigh and pine in the wake of beautiful women, as futile and impalpable as a gust of summer wind. [*He picks up his pack.*] Ho, ho! Now, will you give me back my hat?

HARLEQUIN. [*With an evident effort at firmness*]   No, not unless Columbine first returns the slipper.

PUNCHINELLO. [*Turning to* COLUMBINE] Madam, I make my last appeal to you.

COLUMBINE. [*Folding her arms*] Not unless Harlequin first returns the hat.

[PUNCHINELLO *looks from one to the other*]

PUNCHINELLO. Come, ladies and gentlemen, I have urgent business elsewhere.

PIERROT. Might I suggest that the simplest way out of the dilemma would be for each of the principal parties to return the pilfered articles at the same exact time.

PUNCHINELLO. Quite so! An excellent idea!

PIERROT. I shall count, and at the word three — Is that satisfactory to everybody?

HARLEQUIN. [*Doubtfully*] Ye—yes.

COLUMBINE. [*Doubtfully*] Ye—yes.

PIERROT. Very well, then. One! [HARLEQUIN *begins to loosen the hat from hid head.*] Two!

MARGOT. [*Stepping forward*] Stop, everybody! You, Mistress Columbine, and you, invisible Mr. Harlequin. Because no matter what you do, somebody's bound to regret it. Don't interrupt me, ma'am, and you, wherever you are, keep your lid on and your mouth shut. I want to put it up to the kind ladies and gentlemen that have been studying this performance and I asks them openly, what should be done at this point? Should Columbine give back the slipper or should she hang on to what she's got? Should Harlequin take off his hat? Personally, my honest opinion is that the question can't be answered to suit everybody, so it's my advice that we ring down right here, and allow everyone to go home and fix up an ending to conform to the state of his own digestion.

PIERROT.   But, you know, we're being paid to finish this thing.

HARLEQUIN.   Paid? We're not working for money. We're working for love.

COLUMBINE.   Love!

MARGOT.   Aw, hell!

CURTAIN

Select National Productions of "The Wonder Hat"

1915 – Carnegie Institute of Technology Drama School | Produced by Thomas Wood Stevens

May 19, 1916 – Chicago Little Theater | Produced by Madame Borgny Hammer

August 21, 1916 – 539 Deming Place, The garden of Mrs. Erich Gerstenberg | Produced by the Society of Midland Authors in conjunction with the actors from the Players' Workshop, NY

August 23-24, 1916 – The Players' Workshop | The first professional performance

November 17-18, 1916 – Arts and Crafts Playhouse, Detroit | Dedicatory performance

April 18-19, 1917 – Chicago Art Institute, Fullerton hall | Benefited the American Red Cross

April 26, 1918 – 46th St and Ellis Ave | Performed by the girls of the Kenwood-Loring School | Benefited the Infant Welfare Society

May 5-6, 1921 – The Little Theater in Denver, CO | Directed by Park French

May 31, 1921 – Grace Hickox Studio in the Fine Arts building | Performed by the Studio Players | Benefited of the Civic Music Association of Chicago

November 20, 1926 – Central High School, Aberdeen, South Dakota

1927 – Freeport, Illinois | Performed by the Winneshiek Players

February 20, 1948 – Dekas at the Chicago College Club (30 N Michigan Ave)

BACK OF THE YARDS

By: Kenneth Sawyer Goodman

CHARACTERS

A PRIEST
A POLICE SERGEANT
A BOY
THE BOY'S MOTHER
A GIRL

Illustrations by Emily Murman

*The Scene is the kitchen of a small flat in the district back
        of the Chicago Stock Yards. It is extremely clean and
        neat. There is a door at the back into a hallway,
        and a door at the right into a bedroom.*

*The Time is about nine-thirty on a warm summer evening,
        and the two windows at the left are open, letting in
        a mixture of street-noises.*

SERGEANT BENNETT, *in his shirt-sleeves, sits near one
        of the windows, smoking a pipe and reading the
        Evening American.* FATHER VINCENT, *in the dress of
        a Roman Catholic priest, sits in one of the straight-
        backed chairs beside the table in the centre of
        the room. He is evidently thinking hard about
        something unpleasant, and from time to time mops
        his face with a handkerchief which he takes from a
        clerical hat lying beside him on the table.*

THE SERGEANT.   [*Taking his pipe from his mouth and
shaking his head.*]   It beats hell! It sure does beat —

THE PRIEST.   Eh? I beg your pardon, Sergeant, I wasn't
listening.

THE SERGEANT.   Beg yours, your Reverence. The tongue
slipped on me.

THE PRIEST.   I didn't catch what you said?

THE SERGEANT.   I was saying, it beats all how they
come to do it. And them decent kids mostly, with good
bringing up, too, and fine hardworking folks back of 'em.

THE PRIEST.   More about it in the evening paper?

THE SERGEANT.   Column and a half. Listen here to the
headlines, will you?

THE PRIEST.   No. I don't want to. It makes me feel sick and old.

THE SERGEANT.   [*Laying down his paper.*]   They're calling us dubs. They're after McWeeney to shake things up all over the place. As if it was his fault! Whose fault is it anyhow? I've seen epidemics of crime before. This here ain't the same thing. It's been happening more or less right along. It hops up where you ain't looking for it. It ain't new and it's new all the time. It ain't like placing the blame for regular jobs. It ain't like dealing with regular crooks. You can't put your finger on it. How the devil — excuse me—

THE PRIEST.   Yes, how the —?

THE SERGEANT.   They got one of this here last bunch anyhow, and they got him good, too. He's at the County Hospital — a kid not more'n nineteen with two chunks of lead in him — unidentified — he ain't opened his head. Not a chance for him. It's all in the —.

THE PRIEST.   I saw him myself this evening, about an hour ago.

THE SERGEANT.   Go on with you, now! You didn't know him by chance?

THE PRIEST.   It was Jimmy Reegan.

THE SERGEANT.   No!

THE PRIEST.   Joe Reegan's boy, that I gave the holy baptism to with my own hands. Red-headed Jimmy that I danced on my own knee.

THE SERGEANT.   It's proud you should be of him and you sticking up for him always. What was I telling you only last week? Wasn't I saying he'd be doing his time yet? Wasn't I now? And a long time at that.

THE PRIEST.   He'll be doing longer time than this State could keep him for.

THE SERGEANT.   What's that you're saying?

THE PRIEST.   He's gone.

THE SERGEANT.   Gone?

THE PRIEST.   Without the final consolation; without a word; without a spark of hope to cheer him.

THE SERGEANT.   God have mercy!

THE PRIEST.   Hush! She's coming back.

THE SERGEANT.   [*In a tense whisper*]   What did you get me over here for? You ain't thinking of Michael, surely?

THE PRIEST.   Hush, now, and put a quiet face on you, Sergeant. It may be that I'm only an old fool after all. [*Enter Mrs. Connors, a cheerful woman of thirty-nine or so.*] It's a late hour you're abroad, my dear.

> [*The two men rise and the sergeant struggles into his coat.*]

MRS. CONNORS.   God save your Reverence! And you, too, Mr. Sergeant. I'd have been back earlier if I'd knowed there was two such old friends waiting for me. Think of it, the clergy and the police both to once.

THE SERGEANT.   [*With labored lightness*]   Where was you all the time?

MRS. CONNORS. [*Taking off her hat*] To the movies with a friend. [*To* THE SERGEANT] Don't cock a jealous eye on me now, Peter. It was with Mrs. Steinbrecker I went, her and her cousin, by way of celebrating the birthday of her first twins, and them dead, poor dears, five years back. [*To* THE PRIEST] Come now, Father, don't look at me like I'd done a black bad thing. You wouldn't grudge a poor widow her squint at the films, would you?

[She hangs up her hat and shawl.]

THE PRIEST. God forbid, my dear. They've their educational value, doubtless.

[THE PRIEST and THE SERGEANT sit down.]

MRS. CONNORS. That they have. You should have seen 'em tonight — clear as the living image itself. The story of the taking of Jesse James. That's the bandit out Kansas way, they tell me.

THE PRIEST. [*Hastily*] I know, I know!

[THE SERGEANT coughs.]

MRS. CONNORS. [*To* THE SERGEANT] What's ailing you?

THE SERGEANT. Nothing. A dry spot in my throat.

MRS. CONNORS. You've been sitting in the draught of the window again. [*Turning to* THE PRIEST] God save us! You've' the look as if someone had laid a cold hand to the back of your neck.

THE PRIEST. I was overheated with running for a street car, a while since.

MRS. CONNORS.   That black coat of yours is cruel hot
this weather. You should get you an alpaca thing like
Father Weaver wears. Sit still the both of you till I fetch a
sup of something.

THE SERGEANT.   Ahem! Thank you kindly.

MRS. CONNORS.   There wasn't anything particular you
come to see me about, was there?

> *[She goes to the cupboard and takes out a large
> pitcher of cold tea and three glasses.]*

THE PRIEST.   No, no! We just dropped in or a friendly
chat with you, Mrs. Connors.

MRS. CONNORS.   *[Setting the tea and the glasses on the
centre table]*   Peter's no stranger to be sure. Half the
nights of the week when he's off duty at the station, I
have him sitting up here with me till I'm yawning my
head off for sleep.

> *[She goes to a small ice-box and opens it.]*

THE SERGEANT.   Whist, now! Do you hear that, Father?
And there's many would say I was an amusing man, too.

MRS. CONNORS.   *[Laughing]*   There's many would say
that you're trying to marry me, Peter Bennett. It's a black
scandal else they'll be making about us.

> *[She comes back with a small piece of ice in her
> hand.]*

THE SERGEANT.   The brass of her! Ain't the women hell
these days with their notions of decency? She'll be asking
me to marry her next.

MRS. CONNORS.   [*Dropping the ice into the pitcher of tea*]   I will not.

THE SERGEANT.   Then, I'll ask you again myself for the fifth time.

MRS. CONNORS.   Have you no shame — before Father Vincent?

> [*She goes to the cupboard and takes out a white china sugar-bowl and three spoons.*]

THE SERGEANT.   Hear her, now!

THE PRIEST.   You might do worse, Mrs. Connors.

MRS. CONNORS.   [*Coming back with the sugar and spoons*]   Go on! What would I want with a husband? I can take care of myself, can't I? What with the money I got in the Savings Bank and what I can make off the shop — and Margaret earning her fifteen a week steady as clockwork — and Michael coming to be a fine man, too.

THE PRIEST.   Aye, and have you got Michael a position yet, Mrs. Connors?

MRS. CONNORS.   Almost!

> [*She pours the cold tea.*]

THE PRIEST.   I've had it on my mind that he should have more steady employment. He should be making his own way by now.

MRS. CONNORS.   Let the lad find his groove. It's no pinch for us to be giving him a bit of help yet awhile.

> [*She adds a generous supply of sugar.*]

THE PRIEST.   It's the danger of idle time on a young man's hands that I'm thinking about.

THE SERGEANT.   [*Taking his glass of tea and stirring it carefully*]   What with crap games, and such like, and the dancing they do these days in some of the halls, and the bunch of loafers hanging around the pool parlors, a saint out of heaven couldn't keep straight without he had steady work, Mrs. Connors. That's what his Reverence means to say.

MRS. CONNORS.   [*Passing a glass of tea to* THE PRIEST] Let be, I'm not worrying my head over Michael. He's a good boy, Michael is.

THE SERGEANT.   Aye, he should be a good boy right enough.

THE PRIEST.   You've been an indulgent mother to him.

MRS. CONNORS.   Was it Michael you came to talk about after all? [*To* THE SERGEANT] What are you both fidgeting at? I might have knowed there was something special for you to bring Father Vincent with you.

THE PRIEST.   The Sergeant didn't bring me, I assure you.

THE SERGEANT.   [*Stalling for time*]   Make your mind easy. It was this way. I was coming up here myself when I met his Reverence in the street below. "Come along," I says, "and have a talk with Mrs. Connors," I says. "Her flat's the coolest place I know outside of a beer-garden." It was nothing else at all.

MRS. CONNORS.   [*Setting down her own tea untasted*] Tell me it right out. Has Michael been hurt? Are you trying to break the news to me?

THE PRIEST.   No, no, no! Don't alarm yourself.

THE SERGEANT.   I give you my word on it.

MRS. CONNORS.   He ain't got himself in any trouble? That ain't what you're trying to tell me?

THE PRIEST.   My dear woman, I know no more about Michael than you do!

THE SERGEANT.   You couldn't tell us when he's like to be home, could you?

MRS. CONNORS.   Then it is him you want to see?

THE SERGEANT.   [*Looking at* THE PRIEST *and beginning to flounder*]   Well, in a manner of speaking.

MRS. CONNORS.   What about?

THE PRIEST.   [*Coming to* THE SERGEANT'S *aid*]   I tell you don't alarm yourself. 'Tis only a bit of business we have with him; nothing important. It can wait.

THE SERGEANT.   Sure it can. We only thought if he came in while we was here we might fix it up with him.

MRS. CONNORS.   [*To* THE SERGEANT]   What was it?

THE SERGEANT.   [*At a loss*]   Well, his Reverence was saying—

THE PRIEST.   I was saying to Sergeant Bennett that there's to be a grand picnic of the Parish schools, Mrs. Connors. Sometime next month it's to be, and I thought if Michael would help me take charge of the boys' sports—

THE SERGEANT.   He's a great hand with the kids.

MRS. CONNORS.   And it was about asking Michael to take care of the boys' sports at a church picnic that you've been pulling long faces for a full half hour, was it?

THE PRIEST.   'Tis the heat, and other things beside Michael and the picnic made me pull a long face.

THE SERGEANT.   Couldn't you tell me, will he be home tonight do you think, Mrs. Connors?

MRS. CONNORS.   Michael's gone to Gary — where a job was offered him. He's been gone about two days now. Tuesday morning he went, and he's not sent me word. It's like enough he'll be back tonight if the job don't suit him, or to fetch him his clothes mebbe, if it's what he wants.

THE SERGEANT.   Ah, well, it's early yet. One way or another he might be minded to come.

THE PRIEST.   We'll sit and chat awhile longer on the chance he does.

MRS. CONNORS.   You can sit awhile and welcome, I'm sure, though you did give me a bad turn just now. What with the accidents we're hearing of every day and the mischief some boys is forever getting into.

THE SERGEANT.   Michael do have the way of taking his own advice mostly.

                  [There is a knock at the door.]

THE GIRL.   [*Outside*]   Mrs. Connors, oh, Mrs. Connors! Are you there?

MRS. CONNORS.   [*Rising hastily*]   There, now, what can she want?

[She goes quickly to the door and opens it. THE GIRL, about seventeen, cheaply but somewhat flashily dressed, enters, visibly excited.]

THE GIRL.   Thanks!

[She looks around as if somewhat dazed.]

MRS. CONNORS.   What ails the girl? Ain't you going to give Father Vincent good evening?

THE GIRL.   [*Scarcely noticing* THE PRIEST]   Good evening, Father. Oh, Mrs. Connors, you got to come with me to Mrs. Reegan's. You got to come quick — right away. They can't do nothing with her.

[THE SERGEANT and THE PRIEST rise.]

THE SERGEANT.   They've told her then!

THE PRIEST.   Hush, man, can't you?

[Neither MRS. CONNORS nor THE GIRL notice THE PRIEST and THE SERGEANT.]

MRS. CONNORS.   What's happened at the Reegan's?

THE GIRL.   It's Jimmy! He's been killed! They've just broke it to her.

MRS. CONNORS.   Killed? Jimmy Reegan killed? Oh, God have mercy! How was he killed?

THE PRIEST.   [*Trying to stop* THE GIRL'S *story*]   Hadn't you better go with her, Mrs. Connors. They'll tell you when you —

MRS. CONNORS.   How was he killed?

THE GIRL. Ain't you seen the papers? They shot him last night. There was a hold-up somewhere over on the boulevards. The guy they tried to stick put up a fight.

MRS. CONNORS. What's this got to do with respectable people like the Reegans?

THE GIRL. I tell you it's Jimmy Reegan that's shot. He was took to the hospital. He couldn't give no name. Nobody knew who he was till Father Vincent and Father Weaver seen him there this evening. He was unconscious. He couldn't say nothing. He died at half-past eight.

MRS. CONNORS. [*Turning on* THE PRIEST] Why didn't you tell me? Why didn't you tell me and me having knowed Molly Reegan since we was girls? What do you mean by sitting there like an image and saying nothing at all?

THE PRIEST. My heart was that heavy I had to take my own time, Mrs. Connors. I'm getting to be an old man.

MRS. CONNORS. You and your way! And your heart! And Molly Reegan crying her eyes out for her boy!

THE SERGEANT. Aye, we was getting around to tell you.

THE GIRL. Ain't you coming, Mrs. Connors? Ain't you coming along?

MRS. CONNORS. I'm coming this minute and Father Vincent with me.

THE PRIEST. No, no, Mrs. Connors! Father Weaver's there already and Joe Reegan himself. That's men enough in one house of sorrow. It's women they want now. By your leave, I'll stay here with the Sergeant for a while.

MRS. CONNORS.   [*Putting a shawl over her head*]   You should come with me I'm thinking.

THE SERGEANT.   There now, my dear, his Reverence knows best.

THE PRIEST.   You can send for me if need be.

MRS. CONNORS.   Have it your own way.

>   [*She goes out and is heard clattering down the stairs. THE GIRL is about to follow her when THE PRIEST stops her.*]

THE PRIEST.   Wait a minute, my lass.

THE GIRL.   Well, what you stopping me for? I got to go back with her.

THE PRIEST.   I want to ask you if you've seen Michael this evening?

THE GIRL.   [*With a quick look at THE PRIEST*]   No, I ain't seen him.

THE PRIEST.   Ah, I thought you might have. Or today, perhaps?

THE GIRL.   How would I see him and me working at the cannery?

THE PRIEST.   I only thought that you and he and Jimmy Reegan were great friends.

THE GIRL.   I was no friend of Jimmy Reegan's. Michael wasn't thick with him either. I told him to keep clear of him — honest to God, I did.

THE PRIEST.   You showed good sense.

THE GIRL.   Is that all you want with me?

THE PRIEST.   If you chance to see Michael, tell him I want to talk with him. That's all. Tell him I'll be here for an hour waiting to see him.

THE GIRL.   [*Jerking her head toward* THE SERGEANT] What's he doing here?

THE PRIEST.   He's Michael's friend. Take my word, we know what's best for him. He'll come to no harm through us.

THE GIRL.   [*Sullenly*]   I ain't going to steer Michael into no pinch. I tell you he ain't done nothing. I don't know where he is at that.

THE PRIEST.   Listen to me now, my girl. I've a strong notion you'll be seeing Michael for all you say. And if it's in your head to be warning him against coming home here, it's his living soul you'll put in jeopardy, as sure as you stand there hearing me. Keep your hands off God's work this night and you'll come to thank the old man that asked it.

> [*THE GIRL goes out. THE PRIEST closes the door and comes back to his chair beside the table.*]

THE SERGEANT.   He'll not come to us now with that young fly-by-night waiting at the corner to give him the tip.

THE PRIEST.   No. I've faith in the girl, and in Michael, too, for the matter of that. I'd not be waiting here else.

THE SERGEANT.   [*Coming over and leaning on the table*] Can't you speak out, your Reverence? You've got in your mind that Michael was mixed up in last night's job?

THE PRIEST.   I'm hardly ready to say that.

THE SERGEANT.   But you heard his mother saying he's been in Gary since Tuesday morning.

THE PRIEST.   I saw him last evening.

THE SERGEANT.   The devil you did! And where was he?

THE PRIEST.   In front of Swarz's Pool Parlor, talking with Jimmy Reegan.

THE SERGEANT.   [*Eagerly*]   Couldn't he meet with Jimmy Reegan by chance and pass the time of day with him? That don't prove nothing, does it?

THE PRIEST.   It may be that I am only an old fool after all, as I said to you before, but I'll not be at ease till we've seen Michael tonight.

THE SERGEANT.   I'll bet my stripes on it, the boy's done nothing crooked. But if it's a scare you want thrown into him, I'm your man, and it's a grand time to do it, too.

THE PRIEST.   It's a pity that it always takes an awful thing like what has just happened to show us the real need.

THE SERGEANT.   The real need of what?

THE PRIEST.   A change in our way of looking at things — our educational systems, our way of dealing with the boys in the street, our police.

THE SERGEANT.   What's the matter with the police?

THE PRIEST.   It's not for an old man like me to say, but I've thought for a long time that there was something lacking. You don't seem to understand rightly what's best for the boys in the street.

THE SERGEANT.   We don't, eh? See here, now! Ninety
per cent of the force was once just what you're calling
the boys in the street. Wasn't I one myself? Don't we
know the poor people and their kids like none of your
long-haired, down-state reformers can ever get to know
them?

THE PRIEST.   You know them too well. Too many
of your patrolmen are stationed in their own home
districts. They have too many friends. Sentiment gets
into it too often. They're too easy on the small beginnings
of mischief that go to make the big ends of crime.

THE SERGEANT.   Are you calling me a man that would
let sentiment interfere with my duty?

THE PRIEST.   I remember once when they complained
to you that the boys were breaking windows in
Eisenthorp's vacant factory building on 46th Street, and
Jimmy Reegan and Michael Connors were among the lot;
I remember what the Lieutenant said when the Anti-
Cruelty people got after him about the way the kids were
treating the stray cats and dogs in the precinct.

THE SERGEANT.   Them's little things to be raking up
against the force surely, at a time like this.

THE PRIEST.   You've known for a long time that half
the pool parlors were running crap tables and three-
quarters of the saloons selling liquor to boys under age,
to say nothing of some that sell it to girls.

THE SERGEANT.   You can't expect a bar-keep to spot a
lad's age every time, can you? Would you have us playing
nurse-girl to all the kids of the world? Would you have us
pinching our friends for the little small things like you're
talking about, when half the time you couldn't prove it

on 'em in court if you got 'em there? Where would we get off? I know there's laws to cover what you've said, but it's up to the Department what laws are important to be pushed.

THE PRIEST.   What are laws for if they're not to be enforced?

THE SERGEANT.   Ask them that made them. Ask the Administration. Don't ask me. I take my orders and do the best I know how. I'm straight, too. I've never took a cent of dirty money in my life, so help me God. And that's something to say if I do say it myself.

THE PRIEST.   It is a great deal to say and its [sic] true I'm sure, Sergeant Bennett, I've great respect for you as a man. But it's not graft or politics I'm thinking of. There's something does more to send boys and girls to hell than either of them. It's the rule-of-thumb way we go at crime for the most part, making a great pother of catching and punishing the old hands at the game and letting slip the little things, slurring them over, hushing them up, passing by all the sprees and gambling and devilment that give the crook his start.

THE SERGEANT.   You're a fine one to be talking; you with the name of being the softest-hearted, easiest-going man in the parish, begging your pardon.

THE PRIEST.   It's come to me all at once that we're both greatly to blame. Sergeant, each in his way. I mean to make a new start — with Michael, tonight, God willing it.

THE SERGEANT.   I say again, I'll bet my stripes Michael had nothing to do with it, but if he had now? Supposing he had? Have you it in your mind to help him, Father?

THE PRIEST.   I have, indeed.

THE SERGEANT.   'Twould put me in a sore place.

THE PRIEST.   You'll do your own duty and what's right by Michael.

THE SERGEANT.   'Twould seem a hard thing to make them both go together.

THE PRIEST.   Hush! What's that?

THE SERGEANT.   [*In a whisper*]   I didn't hear nothing.

> [*They both listen expectantly. There is a slight shuffling outside. The door opens and THE BOY enters. He is about eighteen or nineteen, rather too well dressed. He looks very drawn and tired, and lets one arm hang limply at his side. He seems a little startled at seeing THE PRIEST and THE SERGEANT.*]

THE PRIEST.   Well, Michael?

THE BOY.   Good evening, Father Vincent. Evening, Sergeant.

THE SERGEANT.   Back from Gary, eh?

THE BOY.   Yes.

THE SERGEANT.   Job didn't suit you or you didn't suit the job?

THE BOY.   Nothing doing!

THE PRIEST.   Good jobs aren't so easy to find.

THE BOY.   No. Where's my mother?

THE PRIEST.   She's stepped out for a little while.

THE SERGEANT.   She's over at Mrs. Reegan's.

THE BOY.   [*Sitting down*]   Of course, I might have known that.

THE SERGEANT.   Then you know what's happened?

THE BOY.   Yes. It was all in the papers. I seen one of the fellers, too, that heard all about it.

THE PRIEST.   It was a terrible thing, Mickey.

THE BOY.   Fierce! Can you tell me, is Jimmy as bad hurt as the papers say?

THE SERGEANT.   You ain't heard, then?

THE BOY.   [*Looking up*]   Heard what?

THE PRIEST.   He's dead.

THE BOY.   Dead? Jimmy Reegan dead?

THE SERGEANT.   That's why your mother's gone over to the Reegan's.

[They are all silent for a moment.]

THE BOY.   [*Pulling himself together*]   When did she say she'd be back? I've got to see her before eleven o'clock.

THE PRIEST.   Listen to me, Michael. When Sergeant Bennett and I heard about Jimmy Reegan, we just thought we'd come over and have a talk with you.

THE BOY.   [*Nervously*]   I don't know nothing about Jimmy.

THE SERGEANT.   It wasn't exactly about Jimmy, either. His Reverence was saying —

THE PRIEST.   That it seemed like a good opportunity to point out one or two things to you, my lad.

THE BOY.   [*Sullenly*]   I haven't got time to sit here and listen to preaching. I've got to see my mother before —

THE SERGEANT.   What are you in such a rush to see your mother for?

THE BOY.   What business is that of yours?

THE PRIEST.   Easy, now!

THE BOY.   I'm going away from Chicago, if you've got to know. I met a feller that was here from Denver, looking for men. They're short of hands in all the building trades out there. I can get a better start and better pay, only I've got to go out with him on the eleven o'clock train tonight.

THE SERGEANT.   [*Rubbing his chin with his hand*]   Oh, ho! So you're going away, are you? Out to Denver.

THE PRIEST.   Denver's a long way.

THE BOY.   They don't give a feller no chance here.

THE SERGEANT.   Maybe you're right. I'm not saying you ain't.

THE PRIEST.   Your mother'll take it hard, your going so far away where she can't tell how you're getting on all the time.

THE BOY.   I can't help that. She'll have no call to worry about me.

THE SERGEANT. [*With the air of hoping to get away from an unpleasant duty*]   Mebbe you'd like a little word with Father Vincent alone, if you're going so soon?

> [*He gets up.*]

THE BOY.   I don't know what about.

THE SERGEANT. [*Buttoning his coat*]   I'll just step around to Reegan's. If your mother ain't needed, I'll send her back to you.

THE BOY.   Thanks.

THE SERGEANT. [*Taking up his cap*]   Good-bye, Mickey.

THE BOY. [*Without looking up*]   Good-bye.

THE SERGEANT. [*Holding out his hand*]   Good luck to you — in Denver.

> [*THE BOY gets up, winces a little as if it hurt him to move and holds out his hand.*]

THE BOY.   Thanks.

THE SERGEANT.   Goodnight to you, Father Vincent.

> [*He goes out. THE PRIEST mops his face again with his handkerchief and seems at a loss for what to say next, THE BOY listens as if to make sure THE SERGEANT has gone down the stairs, hesitates, and then seems to make up his mind.*]

THE BOY.   Father Vincent, do you know anything about medicine?

THE PRIEST.   Eh? What's that?

THE BOY.   Do you know anything about fixing hurts; I mean fixing them temporary like, bandaging and such, so the dirt won't get into them?

THE PRIEST.   A little, yes, I can do that much. But who's been hurt?

THE BOY.   [*Rather desperately*]   Me. It's nothing. I mean it ain't much.

THE PRIEST.   How?

THE BOY.   It was this afternoon. One of the fellers out at Gary had a gun. We were fooling with it and it went off.

THE PRIEST.   [*Drawing his chair toward* THE BOY *and watching his face closely*]   Where did it hit you?

THE BOY.   In the arm.

THE PRIEST.   Why didn't they take you to a doctor?

THE BOY.   [*Sullenly*]   We was afraid we'd get pinched for having the gun. I tore a piece off my shirt. It didn't bleed hardly at all. I said I'd see a doctor when I got in town.

THE PRIEST.   But you haven't.

THE BOY.   I met the man from Denver that I was telling you about. I wasn't thinking much about it.

THE PRIEST.   Your mother will be back shortly. She'd better have a look at it, too.

THE BOY.   [*Taking off his coat with evident pain*]   I'd sooner she didn't know. She'd be keeping me from doing what I want.

[THE PRIEST helps THE BOY with the coat, swiftly unwinds the clumsy bandage from his arm and glances at the wound.]

THE BOY.   Well?

THE PRIEST.   It's worse than you told me, Michael.

THE BOY.   [*Almost fiercely*]   No it ain't!

THE PRIEST.   [*Putting his hand on* THE BOY's *head*]   I'm afraid it is beginning to fester already and you've got a fever, my lad.

THE BOY.   I tell you it don't hurt much and I ain't got a fever.

THE PRIEST.   Hadn't you better go with me to a doctor?

THE BOY.   There ain't time. I've got to catch the eleven o'clock train. It's after ten now. Can't you help me wash it and put on a new bandage before mother gets back?

THE PRIEST.   [*Standing squarely in front of* THE BOY *and folding his hands behind his back*]   You were never in Gary at all, Michael Connors.

THE BOY.   [*Drawing back*]   Who's told you that lie?

THE PRIEST.   Nobody. I saw you myself last night.

THE BOY.   [*Frightened*]   When did you see me?

THE PRIEST.   Sometime early in the evening. I don't rightly know just what the hour was, about eight o'clock I think, and you were with Jimmy Reegan.

[He takes a bowl from the shelf and fills it with warm water from the kettle on the stove.]

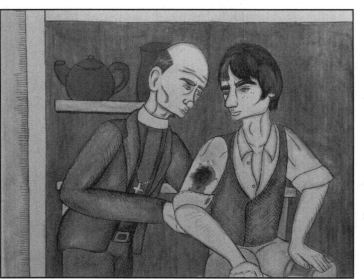

THE BOY.   What if I was? I don't have to account to you for where I was all the time, do I? Or who I talked to, either?

THE PRIEST.   No, I suppose not. But it would be better if you could.

> *[He takes two clean dish-towels from the rack and places the bowl on the table.]*

THE BOY.   I tell you I only seen Jimmy for a minute. I don't know where he went afterwards or what he done. I only know what I read in the papers and what's been told me.

THE PRIEST.   Aye, but I'm afraid you do know more Michael. I'm sorely afraid you do.

> *[He bathes THE BOY'S arm with warm water from the bowl and binds it up with one of the dish-towels.]*

THE BOY.   What's the good of my talking if you ain't going to believe me?

THE PRIEST.   Tell me the truth, lad, and I'll believe you fast enough.

THE BOY.   What makes you think I ain't telling you the truth?

THE PRIEST.   You gave yourself away, Michael, the minute you came in at that door.

THE BOY.   How?

THE PRIEST.   By knowing it was Jimmy Reegan had been shot and not knowing he was dead. His name wasn't in the papers at all. No one knew it was Jimmy till Father Weaver broke the news to his family. There, now, can't you see it's no use lying to me? How could you have known it was Jimmy?

THE BOY.   [*Lying desperately and sullenly*]   I wasn't with him. I had it from one of the fellers, I swear I did. I ain't done nothing. Can't you take my word for it?

THE PRIEST.   I'd be a happy man this night if I could.

THE BOY.   What do you want me to say?

THE PRIEST.   [*Taking a little cross from his own neck and holding it out to* THE BOY]   Can you swear to me on this, Michael?

> [*THE BOY takes the cross and holds it in his hand with his head bowed over it, staring at it as if fascinated.*]

THE BOY.   [*Without looking up*]   You'd ought to take my word.

THE PRIEST.   If you've done nothing, 'twill do you no hurt to swear by the cross, lad, and you'll ease a poor heart that wishes you well, Mickey.

THE BOY.   I — I — [*He looks up suddenly, his face twitching, and reaches for* THE PRIEST'S *hand.*] Oh, Father Vincent, you'll not split on me. You've had it out of me like I don't know what. You've dragged it out of me like you had hot pincers in your hand. I'm sick or you wouldn't have got it from me so easy.

THE PRIEST.   [*Soothingly*]   There, there! Go on, go on. Tell it all to me and we'll see what's to be done.

THE BOY. [*Stumbling along incoherently*] I never
did nothing like this before. I've run with a bad bunch,
I know that, but they knew I was straight — leastways
straighter than they was. They never tried to pull me in
on any crooked stuff, honest to God they didn't. Jimmy
was white to me, too. There was five of us together
yesterday. We got too many drinks. I don't know how
many. Then somebody said: "Let's go to a show," but
we didn't have no more money. Then, somebody else
said: "Let's go out and get some easy coin on the
boulevards." It was all sort of foggy from that on. We
went somewheres and got four guns they had hidden in a
barn. Then one of them that wasn't very drunk went and
sneaked a car out of a garage and picked us up around
the corner. I don't remember where we drove to, till we
came along side of a guy on the sidewalk. I didn't think
what they was going to do, honest to God I didn't. Me and
Jimmy and the other feller in the tonneau jumped out,
Jimmy runs up to the guy on the sidewalk and shoves
a gun in his face. It wasn't even loaded. None of them
was except the one I had and I never took that out of
my pocket. Before we could say nothing, the guy pulls
a gun himself and lets Jimmy have it twice. Somebody
yells "Cops" and we runs for the machine. I knew they
was plugging at us but we didn't plug back. Just as I got
my foot on the step something hit me in the arm. I didn't
think of Jimmy till we'd got clear away. We couldn't go
back for him. The feller that was driving the car had
nerve all right. He took us out to a place in Englewood
and ran the car back to the garage. It wasn't out more'n
an hour. Nobody spotted that he had it out. That's all that
happened.

THE PRIEST. I won't ask you who the other boys were.

THE BOY. [*Miserably*] I wouldn't tell you that.

Nobody'll get 'em. They're safe by now. I wouldn't have said nothing to you either, only walking made my arm come on to pain something fierce. I wish to God I hadn't opened my head.

THE PRIEST.   You shouldn't wish that.

> *[THE PRIEST has finished with the bandage and the boy has managed to get back into his coat.]*

THE BOY.   I do.

THE PRIEST.   Why did you come here?

THE BOY.   To see my mother. I sort of had to see her and say good-bye before I went. I had to get a little money from her.

THE PRIEST.   Then you are thinking of going away?

THE BOY.   *[Pointing to his shoulder]*   I got to go somewhere. I can't hide this thing around here.

THE PRIEST.   You'll go with me now to a doctor and then around to the station and give yourself up.

THE BOY.   *[Startled]*   What are you talking about? What kind of a boob do you take me for?

THE PRIEST.   It's the only way you can make things square.

THE BOY.   *[Defiantly]*   I ain't asking to make things square. I didn't do nothing. They ain't got nothing on me, if you let me alone.

> *[He gets up and makes a move toward the door.]*

THE PRIEST.   *[Stepping between him and the door]*

You'll stop to see your mother. You'll have a word with her.

THE BOY.   No, I've changed my mind about seeing her. I'll trouble you to let me by, Father.

THE PRIEST.   [*Holding his place*]   It's only a short way you'd go, Michael.

THE BOY.   What do you mean by that? You wouldn't put them on to me? You daren't do it. You wouldn't play me a low trick like that. You had it from me like it was in Confession.

THE PRIEST.   Oh, God, why do you tie my hands?

[He steps away from the door.]

THE BOY.   [*With an attempt to smile*]   I'd wish you good-bye, Father Vincent, and thank you kindly for the bandage.

[He holds out his hand to THE PRIEST.]

THE PRIEST.   [*Taking* THE BOY's *hand*]   God go with you, Michael.

> *[THE BOY turns to the door, opens it and comes face to face with THE SERGEANT who stands on the threshold, his hands on his hips.]*

THE SERGEANT.   Well?

THE BOY.   [*Drawing back startled, but still trying to face it out, not quite sure that* THE SERGEANT *has overheard*] Oh, it's you, is it? Did you fetch mother back with you?

THE SERGEANT.   I did not. I ain't been off the landing. I ain't had my ear away from this door.

THE BOY.   [*Turning on* THE PRIEST]   Then it was a dirty trap you set for me after all — you with your fine snivelling talk about being my friend. You're a fine priest! You got it out of me like it was in holy confessional and him listening at the door all the time, with you knowing it. It was a game, a dirty low game you put on to me!

THE SERGEANT.   Shut your mouth, you young ruffian!

THE PRIEST.   Easy, now, Sergeant! He doesn't know what he's saying.

THE BOY.   You're a pair of spying Judases, the both of you.

THE PRIEST.   Listen to me now, Michael.

THE BOY.   I will not.

THE SERGEANT.   You'd do well to keep a civil tongue and listen to Father Vincent.

THE BOY.   [*Sneering*]   What more has he got to say to me?

THE PRIEST.   You'll go with Sergeant Bennett and me to the station, Mickey, and give yourself up. We'll stand by you. It's the only thing to be done.

THE BOY.   A fine lot of standing by me you'll do.

THE SERGEANT.   Come with me now.

THE BOY.   [*Desperately*]   Get out of that door, you big boob.

[*He reaches to his pocket and draws a gun.*]

THE SERGEANT.   [*Making a lunge for him*]   You would, would you?

THE PRIEST.   [*Springing between them*]   For the love of heaven, have a care, both of you!

THE BOY.   [*Covering the sergeant with the gun and almost shrieking*]   Don't you come near me! Don't you put your hands on me!

THE SERGEANT.   [*Losing his temper*]   You young devil, you'd not have got the drop on me like that if I'd of had my gun with me.

THE PRIEST.   Steady, Sergeant! 'Twill do you no good to talk to him like that. [*To* THE BOY] Give me the gun.

THE BOY.   I will like hell!

THE SERGEANT.   [*Regaining his coolness*]   Give the gun to Father Vincent, you fool! Would you only make things worse for yourself?

THE BOY.   Get out of my road. What call have you got to pinch me? They'd have nothing on me only for you two. I'll get out of town and stay out. Let me off, can't you? Who's to know that you done it? Let me off!

THE SERGEANT.   [*In doubt*]   Isn't he mebbe beginning to talk sense now, your Reverence?

THE BOY.   [*Seeing a ray of hope*]   Let me off I say, and you'll never regret it! Honest to God you won't!

THE SERGEANT.   [*Beginning to weaken*]   It would be a hard thing for me to know I'd had a hand in sending the lad up to the pen, your Reverence. And it's only a small thing he's done after all, and little harm intended.

THE PRIEST.   Shame on you, Sergeant Bennett, for saying that.

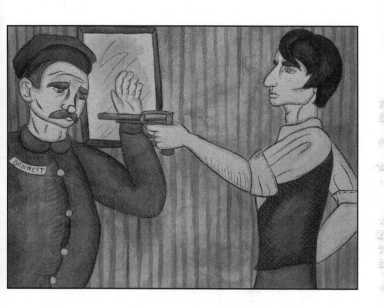

THE SERGEANT.　　Mebbe we can look at things different and both of us be right. I wouldn't be hard on him. 'Tis the first time by his own account.

THE PRIEST.　　'Tis not what he's done already, but what he'll do yet if we let him go his own road with one crime hanging around his neck, that I'm thinking about. There's no two ways of looking at it.

THE BOY.　　THE BOY. [*To* THE SERGEANT]　Don't you listen to what he's saying. You always was more a friend to me than he was.

THE SERGEANT.　　[*Shaking his head*]　If he only hadn't pulled a gun on me!

THE BOY.　　Where would you get off with my mother? You couldn't pinch me! Not on her account, you couldn't! You'd have a swell chance with her after that.

THE SERGEANT.　　[*His pride hit*]　Let be! You'll put down that gun now and come along to the station.

[He makes a move toward THE BOY.]

THE BOY.　　[*Drawing back*]　Stand off, you big stiff, or you'll get yours. I give you fair warning.

THE PRIEST.　　Would you only make things ten times worse than they are for us?

THE BOY.　　[*Half sobbing*]　I don't give a damn. He'll get out of my road. He'll leave me go or I'll give him a dose of what they gave Jimmy. He ain't going to stop me, nor you either.

THE PRIEST.　　We'd not be your friends if we didn't try.

THE SERGEANT. [*Folding his arms*] By God! Father Vincent's right. How far would you get before I put in a call? Not far, I'm thinking, with that arm. They'd get you in an hour at most. Like as not you'd be fool enough to put up a fight, too, and get plugged. They'd be none too careful with you, not them.

THE BOY. Damn you, you've no call to put them on to me.

THE SERGEANT. Supposing I didn't, what good would that do you? You ain't the one to take a lesson from what's happened. I'd only be turning you loose to make a real crook of yourself.

THE BOY. There's worse things in the world than crooks. There's lying priests and dirty scum like you, and —

THE SERGEANT. I tell you once more, put down that gun.

THE BOY. I'll blow your head off if you touch me.

> [*THE SERGEANT and THE BOY stand facing each other, each waiting for the other to make a move.*]

THE PRIEST. Murder's a far worse thing than being only an accomplice in a poor attempt at highway robbery, Mickey. Have you thought of that? No, I don't think you've had the time. You're seeing things wrong tonight. Put away the fear of disgrace now, and the thought of prison. The one will pass when you put your hands to clean work, and the other will be short. It'll go by like a bad dream and you'll come out of it whole, with God's help. It's where you're standing now that I'd have you

see clearly before you put out your feet onto the black
road of death. There's a pit at your toes, lad, a thirsty pit
that sucks men down under the red bowels of the world.
You'll not come back out of it with murder on your soul,
nor look at the stars again nor hear your mother's voice
speaking to you; not when the seas have gone dry even,
or the heavens shrivelled up like a bit of dry parchment.

THE BOY.   There ain't no hell. You can't frighten me like
that.

THE PRIEST.   [*Patiently*]   Have it your own way. But
did you ever think what sort of a life a murderer has
to drag on with even if he's let to live? Not weeks and
months of wishing he was out in free streets like other
men with his friends to give him good-morning and
good-evening, but years, and tens of years of wishing and
wishing.

THE BOY.   What are you giving me? I ain't going to
murder anybody. I ain't going to hurt him if he lets me be.
Leave off clacking at me.

THE PRIEST.   Go with Sergeant Bennett, Michael.
They'll not be hard on you for the first offense. 'Tis only
just penance you'll be doing and, when you're through,
I give you my solemn oath I'll see that you get an honest
start in the world.

THE SERGEANT.   [*to* THE BOY]   You've heard his
Reverence talking sense to you. Come along with me
quiet-like and it will only be a year you'll get at most,
with us to give you a good character, or six months in the
Bridewell mebbe, with parole for part of it.

THE BOY.   I'm not taking any chances of what they'll
give me.

THE SERGEANT.   [*Starting for* THE BOY *in earnest*]
Come on, you fool, before I break every bone in your
body.

THE BOY.   [*Kicking a chair between them*]   Get away
from me! Get away, I tell you!

THE SERGEANT.   Would you now?

> [THE BOY *dodges around the table,* THE
> SERGEANT *follows and grapples with him.* THE
> BOY *wrenches his right arm free and presses
> the revolver to the sergeant's body.*]

THE BOY.   [*Screaming with hysteria*]   Leave go! Leave
go, damn you! Leave go!

THE SERGEANT.   [*Grunting with his exertions*]   Cut it
out! Drop it!

THE BOY.   [*Screaming still louder*]   Let go! Let go or I'll
kill you! So help me, I will!

> [THE PRIEST *is trying to drag* THE SERGEANT
> *away. He only succeeds in hampering him and
> adding to his danger.*]

THE SERGEANT.   [*Now thoroughly angry and shaking off*
THE PRIEST]   Ah, ha! My beauty! I'll get you now!

THE BOY.   I give you three. I give you three to stand
away from me.

THE PRIEST.   [*Wringing his hands*]   Oh, Mary, have
mercy!

THE BOY.   [*Struggling, with his revolver still pressed to*
THE SERGEANT'S *side*]   Don't make me do it! One!

[They stand almost still, gasping for breath.]

THE SERGEANT. [*Snarling*] Drop it!

THE BOY. Damn you, then, two!

THE SERGEANT. [*Their faces are not more than a couple of inches apart*] Drop it, I say.

THE BOY. Three!

> *[They are absolutely motionless for a moment. Then the gun falls to the floor with a clatter, THE BOY relaxes in THE SERGEANT's arms, sobbing.]*

THE BOY. I couldn't! I couldn't! My nerve's gone!

THE PRIEST. No, Michael, my dear, it's only just come back to you.

> *[He takes THE BOY by the shoulder and helps him to the chair by the table. THE BOY buries his face in his arms.]*

THE BOY. [*Sobbing*] I'm a coward! I'm a coward! I couldn't do it! I couldn't! I'm a coward!

> *[THE PRIEST pats THE BOY's shoulder. THE SERGEANT stands beside them, panting like a bull.]*

THE PRIEST. No, no, my lad, my little Mickey, be easy now!

> *[There is a clatter on the stairs.]*

THE BOY. I couldn't! I couldn't! I couldn't!

*[MRS. CONNORS enters and looks around,
    frightened.]*

MRS. CONNORS.   For the love of God, what's happened
now? Tell me, what are you doing to the boy? Can't you
speak, none of you, and tell me what's happened?

THE PRIEST.   Nothing that will do you any hurt in
the end, Mrs. Connors. The worst is over now, God be
praised. 'Twill all come right in a short while. You've no
great call to worry yourself. Take my word.

CURTAIN

Select National Productions of "Back of the Yards"

December 9, 1917 – 1258 W Taylor St , Players' Club of the Chicago Hebrew Institute | Directed by Lester Alden

January 1919 – Performed by the Great Northern Players

October 20, 1925 – Goodman Theater | The theater opening and memorial to Kenneth Sawyer Goodman

January 29, 1967 – Deer Path School | Produced by Louis Ellsworth Lafflin Jr. | Benefited the Lake Forest/Lake Bluff Committee for Family Guidance